▶ Radical Decision Making

Other Palgrave Pivot titles

Bjørn Møller: Refugees, Prisoners and Camps: A Functional Analysis of the Phenomenon of Encampment

Emily F. Henderson: Gender Pedagogy: Teaching, Learning and Tracing Gender in Higher Education

Mihail Evans: The Singular Politics of Derrida and Baudrillard

Bryan Fanning and Andreas Hess: Sociology in Ireland: A Short History

Tom Watson (editor): Latin American and Caribbean Perspectives on the Development of Public Relations: Other Voices

Anshu Saxena Arora and Sabine Bacouël-Jentjens (editors): Advertising Confluence: Transitioning the World of Marketing Communications into Social Movements

Bruno Grancelli: The Architecture of Russian Markets: Organizational Responses to Institutional Change

Michael A. Smith, Kevin Anderson, Chapman Rackaway, and Alexis Gatson: State Voting Laws in America: Voting Fraud, or Fraudulent Voters?

Nicole Lindstrom: The Politics of Europeanization and Post-Socialist Transformations

Madhvi Gupta and Pushkar: Democracy, Civil Society, and Health in India

George Pattison: Paul Tillich's Philosophical Theology: A Fifty-Year Reappraisal

Alistair Cole and Ian Stafford: Devolution and Governance: Wales between Capacity and Constraint

Kevin Dixon and Tom Gibbons: The Impact of the 2012 Olympic and Paralympic Games: Diminishing Contrasts, Increasing Varieties

Felicity Kelliher and Leana Reinl: Green Innovation and Future Technology: Engaging Regional SMEs in the Green Economy

Brian M. Mazanec and Bradley A. Thayer: Deterring Cyber Warfare: Bolstering Strategic Stability in Cyberspace

Amy Barnes, Garrett Wallace Brown and Sophie Harman: Global Politics of Health Reform in Africa: Performance, Participation, and Policy

Densil A. Williams: Competing against Multinationals in Emerging Markets: Case Studies of SMEs in the Manufacturing Sector

Nicos Trimikliniotis, Dimitris Parsanoglou and Vassilis S. Tsianos: Mobile Commons, Migrant Digitalities and the Right to the City

Claire Westall and Michael Gardiner: The Public on the Public: The British Public as Trust, Reflexivity and Political Foreclosure

Federico Caprotti: Eco-Cities and the Transition to Low Carbon Economies palgrave▸pivot

Radical Decision Making: Leading Strategic Change in Complex Organizations

Domagoj Hruška
Assistant Professor, University of Zagreb, Croatia

palgrave macmillan

DOI: 10.1057/9781137492319.0001

RADICAL DECISION MAKING
Copyright © Domagoj Hruška, 2015.

All rights reserved.

First published in 2015 by
PALGRAVE MACMILLAN®
in the United States—a division of St. Martin's Press LLC,
175 Fifth Avenue, New York, NY 10010.

Where this book is distributed in the UK, Europe and the rest of the world, this is by Palgrave Macmillan, a division of Macmillan Publishers Limited, registered in England, company number 785998, of Houndmills, Basingstoke, Hampshire RG21 6XS.

Palgrave Macmillan is the global academic imprint of the above companies and has companies and representatives throughout the world.

Palgrave® and Macmillan® are registered trademarks in the United States, the United Kingdom, Europe and other countries.

ISBN: 978–1–137–49232–6   EPUB
ISBN: 978–1–137–49231–9   PDF
ISBN: 978–1–137–49230–2   Hardback

Library of Congress Cataloging-in-Publication Data is available from the Library of Congress.

A catalogue record of the book is available from the British Library.

First edition: 2015

www.palgrave.com/pivot

DOI: 10.1057/9781137492319

> *You've heard that it was said, "Love your neighbor and hate your enemy." But I tell you: Love your enemies and pray for those who persecute you.*
>
> Matthew 5:43–44

To the most radical leader of all time

Contents

List of Figures	vii
Acknowledgments	viii
Introduction	1
1 The Radical Decision	12
2 Leading Complex Organizations	23
3 Building Mental Models for Effective Leadership	40
4 Driving Radical Change	63
5 The Loadstar	84
6 Taking a Radical Decision	103
7 Rhetoric of Radical Change	116
Bibliography	135
Index	148

List of Figures

1.1	Types of organizations in respect to radical change	19
1.2	Process of radical decision making	21
2.1	Strategic tensions	34
3.1	Levels of knowledge—from journeyman to master	62
4.1	A leader's attitude toward the object of radical change	82

Acknowledgments

Thanks are due to the individuals and publishers concerned for permissions to quote passages from the following works: Sinergija, Zagreb, in respect to *Iluzija strategije* by Darko Tipuric and *Majstor i kalfa* by Zoltan Barackai, Jolán Velencei and Viktor Dörfler.

Introduction

Abstract: *Hruška offers an original insight into the genesis and implementation of radical change. The germ of the book is the notion that we do not know how leaders devise ideas which, at the time they are conceived, most people find crazy and how they eventually make others believe in them. The book goes against the conventional view on the issues of leadership and change management. Hruška avoids using the "cook book" approach to business problem solving by focusing on the two-way effect of how individuals cope and interact in social systems. The focus on the ongoing adaptation and adjustment that an individual goes through provides a more pragmatic and more realistic approach to organizational life than much of the mainstream literature.*

Keywords: interaction; problem solving; radical decisions making

Hruška, Domagoj. *Radical Decision Making: Leading Strategic Change in Complex Organizations.*
New York: Palgrave Macmillan, 2015.
DOI: 10.1057/9781137492319.0004.

When I began my research on radical change some seven years ago, I wanted to make sense of radical shifts in people's lives and the organizations they constitute. This book summarizes the results of my research. The germ of this book was the notion that we do not know how leaders devise ideas which, at the time they are conceived, most people find crazy and how they eventually make others believe in them.

The focus of the book is on the interconnection of decision making and social interaction in forming patterns of strategic change. The book goes against the conventional view on the issues of leadership and change management. Although I am aware that the literature is no doubt rife with people making similar claims, there are six specific features of the book that put together, in my opinion, differentiate the title from the mainstream approach.

The book is focused on the portrayal of the original process of radical change in complex organizations. The approach is synthesized by a number of theoretical frameworks from cognitive, social and organizational psychology. It focuses on three very specific, related topics: how leaders construct mental models which they use to interpret flow of experience (drawing from Neisser 1976; Rumelhart and Norman 1988; Simon 1997; Daft and MacIntosh 1981; March 1994); how leaders generate a governing metaphor which is a cornerstone of a radical mental representation (based on work of James 2007; Weick 1995; Schön 1991; Bruner 1986); and how leaders influence others to accept their radical mental representation (using theoretical frameworks developed by Weick and Quinn 1999; Smircich and Morgan 1982). Whilst many of the approaches currently available for the consideration of strategic change management provide explanatory value at one phenomenological level of inquiry or another, none provides a consistent framework that links leaders' mental processes of developing representation of change to mental processes of other organizational members.

The book advocates the position that the research in the area of business administration is about helping practitioners to solve problems. Problems are constructions of the mind. They always consist of several well-known and several less-known concepts. These concepts are never derived from only one discipline; they cut through areas of study and functional divisions. In other words, doing business is not about functions of marketing, accounting, operations management or finance. Business problems are transdisciplinary. The book takes this into account and addresses phenomena of the radical decision making in complex business settings from the transdisciplinary perspective. It draws from numerous disciplines: philosophy, social, cognitive and organizational psychology, sociology, anthropology and several business administration fields. The three main themes of the observed phenomena mentioned here are used as nodal points around which I organize the examination of a variety of cognitive and social-psychological topics germane to leadership and change management. The book acquires needed theoretical frameworks from different fields to wrestle the phenomena in hand successfully and does not explain different doctrines in detail.

Much of the today's business administration literature is characterized by the "cook book approach." The book before you takes a different angle and deals mostly with the causes and less with the consequences. I adapt the process thinking perspective to organizational studies which is becoming progressively prominent in its implication for organizational and managerial theory (Pettigrew and Fenton 2000; Weick 1995; Tsoukas and Chia 2002; Chia 1999; Van de Ven and Poole 2005). Drawing upon philosophers such as William James (2007) and Alfred North Whitehead (1997), writers in this area of organizational research work from an ontological viewpoint of the world as a process. Entities are hence results of the processes rather than that they exist prior to them. In a nutshell, I use more verbs than nouns.

Further on, numerous books in the field use the macro level of analysis for describing strategic change phenomena, offering advice to enable change (e.g., communicate for buy-in to your vision, build the change management team, generate short-term wins), but they do not get into the process that an individual goes through, which is the key to making it happen. In my understanding, successful organizational change is all about changing individual mindsets. The primary concern of the book is therefore to tap into what is going on in the minds of the individuals that constitute an organization.

Thinking is only one part of the picture; the second is an action. The book is focusing on a particular kind of work—interaction. Interaction occurs as two or more subjects have an effect upon one another and form the basis of social relations. By dealing with the two-way effect of how individuals cope and interact in the social systems, the book offers in my opinion more pragmatic and more realistic approach to organizational life than much of the mainstream literature that considers merely a one-way causal effect.

For the investigation of the relation between interaction and creation of meaning, I use Weick's (1995) approach that he refers to as "sensemaking." The book is concerned with the ongoing adaptation and adjustment that an individual goes through while accepting the radically changed approach to the situation. Although these adjustments may be small, they also tend to be frequent and continuous, which means they are capable of altering structure and strategy. In this way, the rich diversity of interactive practices emerges as a macro pattern that forms temporal strategic and structural stability which in turn enables people to focus their efforts in pursuing novel organizational purpose.

The book offers an unorthodox set of vocabulary for the key terms of observed phenomena. Conventional terminology, in any field, is too often tedious and ineffective. The thing is that words have specialized meanings in a particular area of study. Specific meanings are embedded in actual relationships within the structures of particular social context. Adopting the terminology from the usual vocabulary of business administration profession forms paradigms which precede thinking. With the use of novel language, unusual for business administration discourse, a reader cannot use shortcuts of understanding (stereotypes) but he needs to ask actively and answer questions. In other words, he needs to think.

So, in order to get a new message across, we need a new vocabulary. The book borrows language from cognitive, social and organizational psychology and philosophy and uses words such as metaphor, mental model or rhetoric. Expressions from the business administration occupation such as vision, idea, environment or organizational culture are avoided. However, since words approximate territory, I do use several terms from business administration discourse. For example, I use the following terms: organization, leadership, change and strategy. These words are used in the book title as well as in the body of the book in order to enable readers to initially recognize the area of study.

Focusing on complexity of organizational practice would guide the reader toward two conclusions. First is that the book uses a micro perspective on the phenomena of radical change, driving from the theoretical frameworks of social and cognitive psychology. Second is that the book does not seek to determine causal relationships that will work every time in the same manner for every organizational activity. The two issues unfold the purpose of the book—to describe processes that lead to successful genesis and implementation of decisions that fundamentally change the way people involved in organizations perceive them. If we understand the process, we can hope to make these kinds of decisions in a more satisfying way.

The book is divided into two principal parts: the first designates the perimeter, defines the fundamental concepts and prepares the ground for the second part. It deals with the most important sources of ambiguity in understanding radical decisions and radical change, briefly describes the process of radical decision making, explores the complexity of organizational life and describes the set of tools that we will be using to deal with the confusion. The second part, comprising the last four chapters, depicts four phases of the process of radical decision making. Altogether there are seven chapters, whose content is roughly explained in the following paragraphs.

Chapter 1 sets out to look at the problem of radical change and radical decisions in social systems. Although the book is primarily about organizational decision making, the radical change might occur in other, larger, systems such as industries and even in whole societies. On the other hand, radical change also happens at a personal level. Distinguishing between these four types of radical decisions allows us to understand the interdependencies of change as well as how the process of radical decision making differs in each case. The second issue tackled at the beginning of the book is the question of idiosyncratic radicalism—to whom is the decision radical? Distinguishing between the leader's perspective and the *status quo* organizational perspective, four types of arenas of change implementation are identified: radical, navigated, leaderless and adaptive organizations. The third issue of the first chapter offers a short description of the processes of radical decision making and radical organizational transformation—the phenomena elaborated in the rest of the book.

The intent of Chapter 2 is to describe the essential elements of organizational dynamics so that they can serve as building blocks in the description of the focal phenomena—process of leading radical change. The second chapter starts with the thought-provoking depiction of the complexity of organizational activity and the current practice of organizational research. These accounts counter the frequent simplifications that can be found in the business administration literature on the subject of how people think and act. Although the chapter has a function of preparing the ground for the things to come, it is given in a succinct form so that it can, hopefully, offer some valuable insights on its own. The chapter brings the reader to the domain of several theoretical frameworks of cognitive science, social psychology and sociology in an attempt of demystifying concepts whose definitions are too often blurred. The four main themes for the introductory chapter are organizations, leadership, change and strategy. In a nutshell, organizations are groups of people that work together to achieve a particular purpose. Leadership is about aligning people to the purpose. Strategy is about how we achieve the purpose. Since circumstances in and around the organization change, leader needs to change ways of achieving organizational purpose. The process is called "strategic change management," and it is viewed from the perspective of organizational sensemaking. The last part of the second chapter deals with the role of leadership in driving organizational change.

Chapter 3 describes the process through which leaders build mental models that govern their actions. Opening with an engaging narrative about the famous inventor Nikola Tesla, this chapter sets readers into the information processing paradigm. The rest of the chapter consists of two main building blocks. First, the reader is introduced to the two research paradigms paramount for the depiction of the processes in hand: managerial and organizational cognition within the business administration area and the personal development theory within the area of cognitive psychology. The research frameworks deal with the ways in which people make sense of the situation and act according to it—how they explore their worlds, develop theories about them, test the theories and use them. After that, we follow the formation of the decision making situation representation as well as our response to the situation through our cognitive apparatus. The chapter covers four main topics: perception, mental models construction, adaptive learning and action. Perception is the first mental activity that is elaborated in the description of the cognitive process of decision making. The chapter continues with the description of the process of mental models development. In this segment, the book focuses to the definition of concepts as mental schemata and their amalgams as mental models. The mental models are refined and made more concrete through the process of learning, which is the topic of next chapter section. Following that, the chapter deals with the interconnection of thinking and action. I refer to the use of these elements in the decision making process and elaborate on the cyclic nature of cognitive comprehension of reality. The last part of the chapter elaborates on how leaders develop competence in the use of the mental models they conceive by reflecting of their experience. The central proposition is how an attribute of experienced professionals in any profession is the development of mental representations that control and sensitive their perception so that they are able to notice the elements of crucial importance for the decision-making situation.

Chapter 4 provides a closer look at defining radical change and setting forward the main characteristics of making radical decisions possible. The discussion is organized around two issues—mobilization for radical actions and the leader's character. The introductory part of the chapter explores the radical thinking style of Apple's Steve Jobs, the leader that fundamentally changed several industries. The next part of the chapter defines the term "radical" in a way that it denotes change in understanding of the organization by the people who constitute it. The third part of the chapter deals with aspects of the radical mental model, which are notoriously inaccurate. Although the inaccuracy has its downfalls, it also brings one important benefit—it increases adaptability of the action, which is of crucial importance to the implementation of radical change. The second issue that this part of the chapter points out is that the leader's radical mental model must be formed with the understanding of enacted meaning of the organization. After the foundations of the radical mental model have been set, we go further and explore attributes of radical change and by that we are getting the insight on driving forces behind radical decisions: deep conviction in the soundness of the radical way, commitment to the pursuit of new governing metaphor, extreme emotional disturbance and the willingness to take risk. The important part of the chapter is concerned with the radical leader's identity. We examine the importance of faith in radical decision making and make a point of what should be the cornerstone of a leader's identity. In the last part of the chapter, we offer a way of looking at the object of change that is the only appropriate way for radical decision making. It is a perspective of loyalty without particular interests which, in the continuum of affection and rationality, I call "irrational optimism."

Chapter 5 presents a discussion of the process in which the new mental representation—of radically changed situation—is initiated. Even if the book does not aspire to answer how the spark of the new concept is inflamed, it does give insights into the adherent steps in the development of the radically different mental image. The chapter unfolds in a way that it first offers insight into the biblical story of the journey of three wise men from the east who sought Christ. The story provides valuable insight into the nature of governing metaphor in the process of conducting radical decisions. The chapter continues with the discussion of the origins of new concepts. Three things are apostrophized. First, the different ideas carry various degrees of novelty for different people—the focus is on the individual understanding of a novelty regardless of his immanent cultural surroundings. The second question is *how* new a concept is—tacking the issue of degree of novelty. Finally, I discuss the origins of novel concepts—their embedding in mental models and the nature of the relation between concepts and conceptual structures. The next section of the chapter deals with the elaboration of the governing metaphor in radical decision making. First, I tackle the use of metaphors in the process of developing organization and management theories. This is seen from different points of view: first from the perspective of the genesis of new concepts, second from the position of organizational development and last from the standpoint of radical decision making. The fourth building block of the chapter deals with the central concept in the process of sensemaking—the guiding metaphor. First, the theoretical framework used for describing the role of a governing metaphor in radical decision making is explained. The meaning is constructed on the basis of one mental schema, one character selected from the overall flow of experience. This part of the text also explains how the governing metaphor is seen from the contextual perspective—as the productive character of meaning construction which has a pivotal role in understanding the specific problem solving an instance. Finally, I address the issue of a leader's choice of radical and adaptive approach to deal with the decision making situation. If the leader tries to change the governing metaphor, he begins the radical decision making process. The new governing metaphor is the leader's loadstar. The chapter consists of depicting genesis of the governing metaphor with accent on its possible origins and then sets further discussion about the nature of a loadstar around one key question— what are ways of extraction of a loadstar from the flow of experience. The context and the governing concept lead to the creation of understanding. At the same time, however, what we extract from the flow of experience depends on the context. That is why this part of the work on loadstar genesis elaborates both—the flow of experience and the ways to breach the flow in search of governing metaphor in the interest of meaning. The last part of the chapter deals with the use of the loadstar in the leadership process. First, we explore the two ways to look at the genesis of the loadstar—as an involuntary or deliberate process. Then we investigate the role of context in the process of various possibilities of the governing metaphor interpretation. Last, I address the issue of the emotional message embedded in the metaphors and its role in the genesis and use of the loadstar.

In Chapter 6, we examine the two connected but separate processes: creation of the radical mental model and the process of its validation—the moment of decision. The first part of the chapter deals with the moment of decision taking—the key moment of the decision making process. At the beginning of the chapter, we dive into the psychology of the defining moments in radical decision situations through the insights from a famous historical event—the invasion of Rome by Julius Caesar in 49 BC. In the second part of the chapter, we explore the two ways of radical mental model formation—intuitional and evolutionary development. Afterward, we focus on the process of construction which is based on three phases: governing metaphor, construction of initial mental representation and construction of developed radical mental model. The leader would most certainly like to be sure about the accuracy of the mental representations on which he is deciding to take action. However, that situation is rarely achieved even in the case of adaptive decision making and especially in the case of radical decisions. The leader is, therefore, reasonably willing to tolerate part of the uncertainty, to suspend the process of sharpening the mental representation and to push to the decision taking phase. The next section of Chapter 6, therefore, deals with the validation of the radical mental model. This segment of the book explains the binary nature of the problem of radical decision taking—*status quo* or the radical perspective. In radical decisions, we do not have several alternatives, and thus, we do not have a classical problem of choice. The nature of the radical decision leads to the creation of a single mental representation of radically changed situation. We have only one option, radically different from the existing one, which will or will not be validated. To validate the mental model is to accept the radical path. After we have constructed and elaborated the radical mental model, we will find that many aspects are foggy and not accounted for. That is why, in order to validate radical mental model, in order to make a decision, we need to infuse the mental model with the spirit of hope. The final part of this chapter elaborates on the origins and consequences of the virtue of hope on the radical decision making process.

Since it is the action that brings cognition into reality, Chapter 7 is focused on rhetoric of implementing radical decisions. Rhetoric is any type of persuasion that is the result of human interaction achieved in other ways than by force or threat. The chapter, therefore, gives practical insight into the ways of persuasion. We begin with the presentation of the role of rhetoric in Abraham Lincoln's rise to the presidency. Besides the introductory part, the chapter consists of five building blocks. The first section of the chapter explores people's resistance to change the *status quo* mental models. Particular attention is given to the leader's role in the process. Since the radical change is about altering the existing system of values and meanings that shape models of cognition and action, the leader's role is to challenge existing assumptions enacted in the organization without causing people's intense defensive reactions. The division of the chapter also identifies four ways to reduce resistance to change in radical decision making. Although the processes of social construction of meaning are ambiguous and difficult to describe, it can be said that there are basically two ways in which the leader can affect people in organizations to combine elements of the flow of experience with contextual framework in the interest of meaning. The influence can start as a belief or as an activity driven process. These two approaches are addressed in next two segments of the chapter. Rhetoric based on beliefs can take the form of argumentation and expectation setting and rhetoric based on action forms of behavioral commitment and manipulation. Particular attention in the preceding part of the chapter is given to the description of the process of rhetoric for radical change. The rhetoric job is based on the interpretation of novel perspective to the other members of the organization whose ways of thinking about the situation in hand will consequently be altered. The chapter segment describes the three phases of the incremental process of rhetoric for radical change. Finally, the chapter describes the *parrhesian* approach to radical rhetoric, a particular rhetoric method which is, in my opinion, most suitable for radical persuasion. Coming from the perspective that leading radical change is about setting the path and getting things done, which demands radical paradigm shift, a change of mind and eventually a change of heart, I argue that the radical leader's most important peculiarity should be truthfulness. Hence, argumentation in favor of the *parrhesian* approach for the implementation of radical decisions is presented.

In forming the approach to the ideas discussed in this book, I owe more than I care to admit to many conversations held over the past years with Darko Tipuric, Zoltan Baracskai and Viktor Dörfler. I would also like to thank the anonymous Palgrave reviewer for comments and suggestions. Casie Vogel and Bradley Showalter at Palgrave have provided valuable support in the process of preparing the manuscript.

1
The Radical Decision

Abstract: *Radical change, a fundamental change in the way people make sense of their surroundings, occurs on individual level, on organizational level but also on the level of larger systems such as industries and the societies as a whole. Hruška describes types of radical change and deals with the question of idiosyncratic radicalism. By distinguishing between the leader's perspective and the status quo organizational perspective, Hruška identifies four types of arenas of change implementation: radical, navigated, leaderless and adaptive organizations. Finally, Hruška examines the four phases of the process of radical decision making and radical organizational change: construction of leader's mental model, search for the new governing metaphor, radical decision taking and rhetoric of radical change.*

Keywords: processes of radical decision making; types of radical decisions

Hruška, Domagoj. *Radical Decision Making: Leading Strategic Change in Complex Organizations.*
New York: Palgrave Macmillan, 2015.
DOI: 10.1057/9781137492319.0005.

Radical change—a fundamental change of the enacted *status quo*

Radical change is about breaking the circle of old routines of thinking and acting, our past life. Radical decision making is risky business, but it is often the only way to reach the goal. It is a fact of life that trying to leap an abyss with more than one jump is not a good idea.

Radical decision making as described in this book gives a rationale for distinguishing strategic and routine behavior through enactment theory. In the business administration context, radical decision is about making a fundamental change in the business model, which requires changes in company strategy, structure and culture. At times, such change can be an effect of an outside disturbance but it can also result from the emergence and the activities within the organization. That is, systems are capable of producing structures that may disturb and alter the very system that produced them. The organizational leadership is in charge of making the disturbances happen. It needs to understand and be able to manipulate with the patterns of complexity. In conducting radical change, leaders are symbols, rather than ship captains navigating their vessels to the port. The complex organizations wobble on the edge of chaos—they are sufficiently active to be dynamic but not so active as to risk recurrent disorder. Radical change occurs when they step over that edge to embrace a fundamentally different identity.

What do we mean when we say that we will make a radical decision? Or that that situation demands radical change? The term "radical" has many meanings, but it always means that some fundamental change is in question. From an etymological perspective, the word comes from Latin *radix* that indicates the root. So, just as roots are crucial for life and fundamental for understanding of the organisms, so the radical decision must be of profound impact and importance. To say that the radical decisions are those that fundamentally change the organization is not good enough. In order to be able to use the concept of radical decision making, we need to know what exactly a "fundamental change" is. In a nutshell, fundamental change is a change of the way in which people understand the organization. It is the understanding of the organization and acting in respect to this meaning that constitutes the organization's "roots."

At first, the term "meaning of the organization" can seem to be vague and hard to define, but it is not. People in every organization have a feeling of "what the organization is all about" or "how things are done around here." The best way to understand the concept of organizational sense is to take a look at the ways through which it is enacted. As we have discussed in the Chapter 2, the word "enactment" denotes the fact that our interpretations generate actions that create challenges to which we have to respond. It is a construct based on both—interpretations and actions.

The medium for radical change, organizational enactment, integrates the perspective that the generic routines and familiar patterns of organizational activity are, usually, reconstructed and reaffirmed by the people's interaction. After the individual interpretations have been enacted and stabilized through the activity, they act as a medium for carrying out all organizational action. Since the organizational enactment is shared, each member of the organization is able to identify his contribution to its construction and, what is more important for definition of radical perspective, he is able to detect changes within the structure. Although the organizational enactment is in a state of constant flux, through the activities of the people that constitute the organization, it is still steady in its fundamental characteristic—its meaning. Of course, people may not fully agree on the perception of the situation in hand, but the thread of coherence in their interpretations and consecutive actions is what keeps the sense of an organizational enactment stable.

The fundamental roles of organizational enactment are threefold—predetermination of future organizational behavior, interpretation of previous experience and initiation of antagonism toward different approaches. A fundamental characteristic of organization enactment, however, drives from the elaborated thesis that organizations choose their environment from a number of options, and then subjectively perceive it. As Starbuck (1976, 1081) asserts, the selection process as well as the process of perception is incremental, spontaneous and strongly influenced by social norms and habits. Since the process is socially constructed, generic routines and familiar patterns of activities tend to recreate and reaffirm the individual's interaction within the organization. Therefore, there is only a slight chance that there will often be a significant divergence in the collective perception of the organization. The fact allows the organizational enactment to be defined as the foundation for radical decision making.

Decisions that do not result in a fundamental modification of organizational enactment are referred to as adaptive decisions. Adaptive change is a conservative approach to the transformation of an organization, based on an attempt to keep as much of the "old" as possible in building the "new." Radical and adaptive decisions are not a question of intensity but a question of sort. Only in implementation, through change of social constructs, as I will discuss in the last chapter, the decision result obtains continuum. Based on the change of the meaning of the organization, a new taxonomy of decisions and organizational change can be put in place. If the leader attempts to change enacted meaning of the organization, the decision to do so is the radical decision. If the change of meaning is successfully conducted and the new meaning is enacted, we can say that radical change took place. In other case, if the decision is about changing the elements of the situation in hand without interfering with its meaning, the decision is called adaptive decision, and it consequently leads to adaptive change.

The taxonomy of organizational decisions, based on change of meaning in the problem solving situation, fits with the taxonomy of decisions based on the level of structure of the problem situation developed by Herbert Simon (1977). While the Simon's taxonomy looks at the present situation it terms of our previous experience, the taxonomy of change of meaning looks at the future in terms of what is going on in the present. The two types of decisions derived from the Simon's taxonomy are programmed and unprogrammed decisions. From an etymological perspective, decision taxonomy of programmed and unprogrammed stems from computing. The program is detailed guidance to the system on how to respond to the complex environment in the performance of a particular task. A set of rules and procedures is by definition a program. Unprogrammed decisions are the ones for which the system has no pre-specified procedures and solutions. In order to solve these situations, the decision maker relies on the general capacity for intelligent adaptive action (37–41). Computer analogy is useful to the decision model because it indicates the term "general mechanism for problem solving," which, unlike the single "program," treats every situation in a specific way. Simon argues the usefulness of programmed decisions through the high cost of usage of the "general problem solving mechanism" and says it is advisable to reserve capacities of that mechanism for decisions that are "truly novel" (47). Within this explication of unprogrammed decisions, Simon gives an indication of taxonomy of decision by the use of "general problem solving mechanism." Change of the central organizational construct—a radical decision—is certainly a decision that requires the use of cognitive mechanisms that Simon defined as "truly novel." Programmed decisions are always adaptive. The meaning of the organization does not change, neither for the decision maker, nor for the social context in which the decision is made. It is not so with the unprogrammed decisions. Poorly structured problems can be addressed with the adaptive and the radical approach. Besides this essential difference, taxonomy of decisions on the basis of change of meaning differs from the classical taxonomy of programmed and unprogrammed decisions on three other important issues. First, it is impossible to say whether it is better to make radical or adaptive decision in a specific situation. Second, the decision to use the existing sense of the situation or to change it is of binary nature—only in the implementation, through change of social constructs, the decision result obtains continuum. Third, decisions become adaptive or radical at the moment of the decision, not in the phases of decision making process which follow the decision moment, as it is the case with programmed and non-programmed decisions. Subsequent chapters will shed more light on these characteristics of radical decisions.

Types of radical change

The radical change takes place in settings that range from the individual level to the level of complex social systems. At least four levels of radical change can be identified: individual as a change of personal identity, organizational as a change of collective identity, industrial as a change of rules of the game and society as a change of ideology.

Individual radical change is about profound and sudden change of identity. Conversions of all kind, especially religious conversions, are best-known individual radical decisions. The decision to "come out" as a gay person twenty years ago or to be an emancipated woman two hundred years ago are also illustrations of radical action. Individual radical decisions depend only on the person making it, in other words, they do not require decision maker's rhetoric effort as other radical decisions do. What constitutes a radical decision depends on the person's identity before the change as well as on his surroundings. Eating a neighbor is perhaps radical for a London vegetarian but not necessarily for a New Guinea cannibal.

Organizations, as groups of people who work together to achieve a collective purpose, are also defined by their identity. Change of collective identity is the business of organizational radical decision making. Organization's identity is enacted in a way "things are done around here" and is constructed by everybody in the organizations; first and foremost, of course, by the decision makers. The organizational enactment is a resultant of one concept that acts as the corner stone of individual interpretations of the organization. If this governing metaphor is altered, we have a radical organizational change. Dutch electronics giant Phillips, for instance, has replaced or re-assigned more than half of the top two hundred managers and put about 1,800 staff through programs with a focus on performance culture in past two years. Another well-documented example is a change in enactment of AOL and Time Warner during their failure of achieving synergy from the 2001 merger. The example of radical organizational change is also Nokia's history of streamlining its businesses over and over since it was founded in 1865. It takes a radical leap from ground wood pulp mill in South-western Finland to the world leader in mobile phones sales that Nokia was fifteen years ago.

Radical change can take place in the context of a number of organizations that strive to achieve the same purpose. Discipline of strategic management defines this context as industry. Same as organizations, industries have rules of the game, *status quo* position, which can be radically altered. Goal of strategic change is position of competitive advantage. Competitive advantage can be achieved by the introduction of disruption within the industry's enacted environment. The fundamental question of the book is how we can generate and introduce such disruptive initiative. Technology changes are pivotal example of such disruptions. The invention of fire and the wheel have indeed radically changed enacted ways of hunting and building at the time. Transition from fuel to energy cars is one of today's radical shifts. Some other examples of radical industrial decisions are: introduction of novel sale channel, like Amazon did; introduction of a novel industry standards, like Microsoft's operating systems based on graphic interface in respect to IBM's command-line interface; change of industry's focus, like Apple did in the mobile phone industry by changing focus from technical features to design. Another good example is the change of practice of insurance companies in respect to alternations in the United States health care system enacted in 2010 by the Obama administration. Outside the business context, in warfare, the radical change was the importance of machineguns in respect to cavalry in the First World War.

Finally, the radical change can take place in the whole society. The culture is influenced by the governing metaphor which forms an ideology—an enacted way of thinking and living which is most visible in the interaction. Such radical shifts were, for example, the rise of Christianity with love as a governing metaphor, the French Revolutions with the idea of *La Liberté* or the communism with the governing metaphor of absence of social classes. These and other ideological shifts are always well documented and as such present a good material for learning about the processes of radical decisions making.

The focus of the book is a radical decision making in complex organizations. Two other social systems—industry and society—can also be seen as organizations. There are, however, certain differences between the two and the organization. The industry is made out of organizations so that industrial enactment tends to be more stable over time than the organizational enactment. The society, on the other hand, has less defined purpose than the organization that causes a decrease in a number of problem solving and decision making opportunities. However, the same logic and the same process apply for each of the elaborated social systems. So far as the individual radical change is concerned, the organizational change happens when people in organizations change their mindsets. That is when they change the ways of how they think and act in any social system. In this way, all radical decisions are primarily individual—if people in the organization change, the organization will change as well.

Idiosyncratic radicalism of leaders and organizations

Besides the explication of the social systems in which the radical decision making takes place, the organizational change can be observed from the perspective of idiosyncratic radicalism of leaders and organizations. In respect to radicalism of the decision from the leader's and organizational perspective four types of organizations can be identified: radical, navigated, leaderless and adaptive organizations (see Figure 1.1).

The decision can be radical for the leader and the organization. Sudden and broad changes in the environment can force people and organizations to change the ways of doing things and force them to find the new solutions. The leader is the one who sees the new paradigm and

	Change is not radical for the organization	Change is radical for the organization
Change is radical for the leader	Leaderless organizations	Radical organizations
Change is not radical for the leader	Adaptive organizations	Navigated organizations

FIGURE 1.1 *Types of organizations in respect to radical change*

persuades the organization to follow him. Such case is the Cherokee leader Sequoyah. According to the US Census of 2010, the Cherokee Nation is the largest of the 566 Native American tribes in the United States. They have assimilated numerous cultural and technological practices of European American settlers including writing. Around 1809, Sequoyah, a Cherokee silversmith who regularly traded with white settlers, and saw advantages of writing, although he spoke no English, began developing a written form of the Cherokee language. Even though the implementation was harsh, by the 1820s, in Georgia, the Cherokee had a higher rate of literacy than the whites around them (Walker and Sarbaugh 1993, 70–94). Only in the case of radical organizations, the entire process of a radical decision making, as described in the book, takes place.

Radicalism of change has an idiosyncratic quality; it is in the eye of the beholder. For instance, in March of 1999, Renault Motors acquired the failing Nissan Motors of Japan. The man who Renault chose as CEO for Nissan, Carlos Ghosn, reduced manufacturing overcapacity, got rid of the seniority system and replaced it with performance-based management and eliminated the keiretsu relations. In 1999, the company had declared its worst loss in its history and in 2000 its biggest profit ever. Although the actions Ghosn undertook are part of every business administration textbook, it was radical for the people in Nissan who were doing things one way for years and then, suddenly, in just a few months, everything changed. In this kind of cases, the leader knows exactly what he is doing; he has a precise map of the territory, and he just has to navigate the organization to its destination.

The leader is an architect as well as a builder of the organizational enactment—the ways in which people in the organization think and act. By the psychology of leadership, the people in organizations replicate patterns of leader's thinking and action. In *Metaphysics* (book 12, section 1075a) Aristotle discusses the relation between leaders and their organizations this way: "For the efficiency of an army consists partly in the order and partly in the general, but chiefly in the latter, because he does not depend upon the other, but the other depends upon him." If the leader is a newcomer to the organization, it might be a while until he fully recognizes all the aspects of organizational enactment. If the organization's *status quo* value system is strong, the "stranger" can be sucked in by the "usual practice." In that case the organization is unable to transform. If the leader accepts the existing governing metaphor of the organization, he is not about to implement radical change. The organization is *de facto* leaderless.

The decision to solve the decision making situation in a way that does not offer novel meaning for the leader or the organization is called "adaptive decisions." Adaptive decisions correct specific aspects of the business model but are not intended to change any of its features fundamentally.

Process of radical decision making

Radical decisions are sometimes necessary, sometimes welcomed and sometimes fatal. The book, however, is not about the outcome of the radical decisions but about how we construct these kinds of ideas and how we implement them. Most of the book focuses on the process of radical decision making. The process is viewed from the perspective of the decision maker and as such, hopefully, will represent a way to increase understanding of radical decision making.

The process consists of four distinctive segments. Each stage is described in one chapter of the second part of the book. First segment of the radical decision making process is concerned with understating of the situation in hand by the leader who is about to try to implement radical change. An understanding of the situation depends on the decision maker's identity. The leader's identity is constructed throughout the ongoing cycle of thinking, action and *ethos*. Sensemaking process is based on one element of the entire flow of experience that is taken as an equivalent of the situation—the governing metaphor. In the first part of the process of radical decision making, the leader identifies the governing metaphor. If the situation is such that demands radical change, the leader will begin the second phase of the process—search for a new governing metaphor, different from the *status quo* reference point. The genesis of a radical governing metaphor is described as a process of concept extraction from the social context through selective attention. When the new mental model, based on the radical (different than the *status quo*) metaphor is constructed, the leader has to validate the model and decide whether he is willing to try to implement it. That is the moment of radical decision taking—third part of the process. Since the radical mental representation is more an outlook than a strict plan of action, the leader has to take a chance and hope the situation will develop in his benefit. If the leader decides to go through with it, he will engage in the fourth phase of the process—rhetoric of radical change. If the implementation process is successful, the situation will be radically altered, and if not, only the adaptive change will take place. The process is presented in Figure 1.2.

Within the defined process of radical change, a separate but connected process happens in the mind of the radical decision maker. The leader's identity provides virtue of hope that in turn enables decision taking. If the leader implements the decision in a specific way, described in the

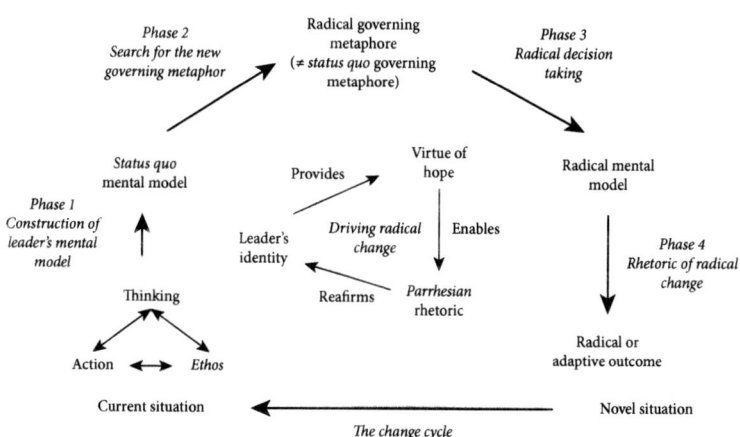

FIGURE 1.2 *Process of radical decision making*

book as the *parrhesia*, his activities will reaffirm his radical identity and allow him to pursue the radical change further.

This leadership cycle of radical change enables organizational transformation which is an iterative process. Iterative changes of organizational enactment through the use of radical governing metaphor can be understood as a process of organizational learning. Intuition, judgment and creativity express the capacity to recognize and react based on experience and knowledge. Without the knowledge, which arises from the experience, understanding of the situation would be made only by small, slow and painful steps. Implementation of radical decisions, therefore, is an active process of reflection on the collective experience, in which decision makers construct and convey novel ideas or concepts based on existing or past knowledge.

The theorizing on radical decision making, what the book is all about, offers insight into the nature of the genesis and implementation of radical mental models. Getting to understanding the nature of radical decisions contributes to the development of business decision making because we are now able to specify appropriate thinking patterns and modes of action. By identification of elements that occur in the process of radical change and by elucidation of their interaction, we can diagnose problems that hamper effective radical decision making.

2
Leading Complex Organizations

Abstract: *The frequent simplifications that can be found in the business administration literature offer false perspectives on how people think and act. Hruška brings the reader to the domain of several theoretical frameworks of cognitive science, social psychology and sociology in an attempt to demystify concepts whose definitions are too often blurred. The four main themes are organizations, leadership, change and strategy. According to Hruška, organizations are groups of people that work together to achieve a particular purpose. Leadership is about aligning people to the purpose. Strategy regards to how we achieve the purpose. Since circumstances in and around the organization change, a leader needs to find new ways of achieving organizational purpose. The process is called strategic change management.*

Keywords: change; leadership; organization; organizational complexity; strategy

Hruška, Domagoj. *Radical Decision Making: Leading Strategic Change in Complex Organizations.*
New York: Palgrave Macmillan, 2015.
DOI: 10.1057/9781137492319.0006.

Reducing perplexity by managing complexity

The trouble with dealing with complexity is that complex problems never yield with a definite solution which can appease our sensemaking apparatus. Complexity is about flux, just as life itself. In a moment of anxiety we could say that our lives are reduced to the futile ongoing activity of making sense of ourselves and the world—on the purposive apprehension of whether we will be able to stop the flux, find the oasis of tranquility from where we can observe and understand.

In order to understand, we want to see the world "as it is," not as it seems to us. We want to be objective about it. The quest for objectivity has described most of the scientific efforts until today, not only in mechanics but in social sciences as well. Scientists urge us to discard all over-romantic egoism and see ourselves "objectively."

But what does it mean to be objective? How should we proceed with our inquiry if we were to do it objectively? Polanyi (1964, 3) voiced the answer in regard to comparison of men with respect to time and space:

> In a full "main feature" film, recapitulating faithfully the complete history of the universe, the rise of human beings from the first beginnings of man to the achievements of the twentieth century would flash by in a single second. Alternatively, if we decided to examine the universe objectively in the sense of paying equal attention to portions of equal mass, this would result in a lifelong preoccupation with interstellar dust, relieved only at brief intervals by a survey of incandescent masses of hydrogen—not in a thousand million lifetimes would the turn come to give man even a second's notice.

Obviously, even the biggest proponents of objectivity do not look at the world in this way. As Chesterton (1908, chap. 4, 11) vividly puts it, "It is quite futile to argue that man is small compared to the cosmos; for man was always small compared to the nearest tree."

Objectivity is not about ousting the man from the central position of the scientific interest. It is about another issue, equally unfortunate in its social science consequences—the cognitive strategy of simplification. In order to objectively comprehend the natural world, science has relied on different cognitive strategies. Descartes was the first to introduce reductionism as a cognitive strategy of simplification, both in terms of examination and in terms of explanation. The reductionist mindset ultimately culminated in the works of Newton, who famously wrote in one of his reflections in a manuscript on rules for correct interpreting of prophecy (Untitled Treatise on Revelation, section 1.1): "Truth is ever to be found in the simplicity, and not in the multiplicity and confusion of things." The Newtonian reductionist paradigm dominated Western science for centuries and still represents the cornerstone of numerous scientific fields ranging from natural to social sciences.

The reductionist paradigm is unable to account properly for sudden massive and stochastic changes that characterize complex systems. Aristotle noted the problem of reductionism in *Metaphysics* (book 8, section 1045a) when he stressed that "[t]he whole is more than the sum of its parts." The whole system can neither be deduced nor reduced from the qualities of its individual parts. The same point is put forward by Levy (1992, 8) when he says, "Reductionism does not work with complex systems, and it is now clear that a purely reductionist approach cannot be applied...in living systems the whole is more than the sum of its parts. This is the result of...Complexity which allows certain behaviors and characteristics to emerge unbidden." Therefore, an epistemological rethink is needed to prompt a paradigm shift from reductionism to the perspective that can address the complexity of social systems.

The study of interactive systems is an area that can significantly benefit from the change of the epistemological perspective of dealing with complexity. The need for tackling complexity in organizational research is put forward by three reasons: the nature of organizational systems, the nature of the human mind and the reach of the existing research apparatus.

First issue is adduced by the fact that social organizations are one the most complex systems. In his hierarchical framework of systems, Kenneth Boulding (1956) arranged systems in a hierarchy of complexity. The hierarchical approach classifies systems into nine levels or entities. According to increasing levels of complexity, each new level brings in a different relation, as well as involving those at previous levels. The nine levels of the hierarchical approach are as follows: frameworks (static structure), clockworks (simple dynamic), thermostats (control mechanisms), cell (self-maintaining structures), plants (pre-determined patterns of growth and decay), animal (increased mobility and self-awareness), human beings (self-consciousness), social organizations (roles, perceptions, status) and transcendental systems (200–201). Therefore, in order to tackle the complexity of organizational life we must abandon the reductionist objectivity and focus on a holistic approach to human experience especially the experience of interaction. As McCarthy

(2001, 286) argues: "There is no ontological reality or pure objectivity waiting to be investigated by a neutral observer. Rather the objects of experience are a social construction based on quasi-transcendental and anthropological interest for continuing the social lifeworld." The problem of coping with organizational complexity is discussed in more detail in the rest of this chapter.

Secondly, as human beings we have to see the universe from the perspective within us and speak about it in terms of personal impressions. Since the subjectivity influences human cognitive apparatus, all complexity of human thinking is inevitably, by the self-regulating process, integrated with the organizational systems. The cognitive processes and their subjective quality are main topic of the book's third chapter.

Thirdly, the strategies and the structures of contemporary business organizations are largely modeled on principles of cause and effect based on linear chains of command. This mechanistic, Newtonian perspective dominates the business administration literature as well. The Newtonian research logic commands that the targets are set prior to the analysis. The accomplishment of goals is, therefore, reflected in the knowledge demanded by the divisions of labor. The division of labor, on the other hand, determines the functions that the organizational agents perform. The performance is motivated by their compensation schemes. As Spender (1998, 15–16) argues, the roles established by the division of labor are afterwards coordinated, first by the system of clear rules, and then by the position of authority which tries to match the behavior of individuals with the requirements of the role. Power is used to keep the behavior of the agents within the frame of the designer's expectations. The power of the chief bureaucrat is legitimized by the authority that is accepted when an individual becomes a member of the organization. The structure of organizational power is explicit in terms of its rules, as well as its rewards and sanctions. Communication problems can appear, mostly due to the inadequate information of employees about their roles. In this regard, the organization has no problem with knowledge. Problems in these kinds of organizations, as Fiske and Taylor (1991, 265–266) note, are decomposed, ignoring the influence of interaction in the process. They are also in motion in reverse schedule—from wanted results to needed preconditions. Decision makers recognize patterns in decision making situations and use simplified rules that they consider appropriate for a particular situation. They simplify complex phenomena by reducing them to the level of numbers (like profit or market share) which they afterwards treat as the equivalent of more complex reality. Finally, they take the current experience in a way that allows them to retain their existing beliefs and their interpretation.

The application of complexity theory in organizational studies would consequently lead to better understanding of how organizations cope with surroundings and the conditions of uncertainty. The issues of correlation and unpredictability post two strong and pervasive elements that constitute the complexity of every interactive system. They are, however, commonly avoided issues in business agendas. It is up to the organizational research to change that. In this perspective, the leading of organizational complexity is less about controlling and more about developing leaders' abilities to influence organizational behavior in ways that enhance the likelihood of industrious scenarios.

Reducing the perplexity of managerial experiences cannot be done by simple tools of reductionism. They need to be tackled with the complex tools appropriate for sophisticated adaptive systems. The demands of this shift for an organizational scholar are well put by Weick (2001b, xi): "To appreciate organizations and their environments as flows interrupted by constraints of one's own making, is to take oneself a little less seriously, to find a little more leverage in human affairs on a slightly smaller scale, and to have a little less hubris and a little more fun"

Dynamics of complex organizations

The dominant perspective of organizational complexity arises from the notion that a number of different kinds of activities are being carried out simultaneously by different people or groups of people. Therefore, there is no single authoritative locus of control that sets tasks and controls results for everybody. In this book, however, another position is taken. The complexity of organizations stems primarily from the fact that it is partly formed by the minds of the people who constitute them. In that respect, even the smallest organizations can be complicated if they are made up of people who construct confronting interpretations of reality. It is not just geographically distributed, multi-cultural and multi-disciplinary organizations that are complex. Even marriage can be a complex organization. On the other hand, an organization that incorporates bigger number of people but with harmonized interpretations is not considered complex.

The two issues that would certainly benefit from the application of complexity theory in organizational studies are the unpredictability of the surroundings and the correlation of elements within the system.

The notion of unpredictability comes from the inability to control the events in the surroundings of the organization. Treatment of the organizational environment by the sequential information processing paradigm emphasizes the idea that the environment is an objective entity. The stance has been emphasized by the reductionist mindset so that the alternative is, usually, overlooked. And the alternative is that, as Weick (1995, 34) argues, "People create their environments as those environments create them."

Organizational theorists, usually, do not deal with the idea that the environment is located in the minds of the organization's agents and that it is imposed on the experience of each of them through their activity. This kind of view of the environment ignores the fact that the object and the subject often have a significant impact on each other, and that the decision making process constructs, extracts or destroys many of the features of the environment. As Weick (1979, 176) argues, the organizational reality described by these terms is relative because the correctness of the decision is dependent on the observation used for its evaluation. Follett (1924, 118–121) alerts us about the issue of circularity of decision making context and actions of the organizational agents when she says that the activity of the individuals are only in a limited sense defined by the stimulus of the situation, since the activity itself helps to define the situation that causes the activity. In other words, as Simon (1997, 13–14) points out, the decision of an individual is not only the product of his mental processes but is also under the influence of organizational dynamics. An extremely important effect of such a process for modeling radical decision making is exactly that there is no singular, monolithic, fixed environment that is separated from the organizational members. Members of the organization define the environment, and the environment defines them in turn. There is no "they," as Weick (1995, 31) argues, which set the environment before us. The word "they" refers to active individuals within the organization whose actions significantly affect the way in which the rest of the people in the organization think and act.

The second issue of complexity is the problem of correlation of elements within the system. In organizations, the problem of interaction that arises is due to the differences of interpretations of the organizational agents.

Interpretation is the key element that distinguishes social organizations from the system of lower complexity. Interpretation is an explanation of meaning of the object of attention. To interpret means to decode events from the environment into categories that form part of a group's culture or language system (Weick 2001c, 72–76). The act of interpretation involves creation of mental maps and representations that simplify the decision making situation in order to enable action.

In the context of organizational research, interpretations are used in explaining the discrepancies and ambiguities of activities of the members of the organization. As March and Olsen (1976, 25) point out, organizations are often incomprehensible precisely because they are woven of many conflicting interpretations of which all are acceptable.

Comprehensive ambiguity that is an essential feature of the organization means that most of what we know comes from the process of interpretation. Interpretations are built through interaction. Smircich and Stubbard (1985, 727) describe the organization through the quality of interaction as a collection of people who share beliefs, values and assumptions that encourage organizational agents to build mutually reinforcing interpretation of their own activities and the activities of others. We cannot manage the organization unless we accept the possible differences in interpretations.

From interpretation point of view, the organizational dynamics can be presented as the flow of experience. Weick (1995, 38–39) notices how members of the organization develop conclusions by intersection of the flow of experience. These conclusions are cognitively arranged in causal maps that predetermine future behavior. Predestination of a certain type of behavior defines the patterns of expectations about the future course of events. So created "rationalities" are included in broader belief systems out of which some are individual and some shared by the group.

The process of interpretation arises from the need of individuals to recognize that there is an external reality in their relationships. Interpretation building is indispensable organizational activity or otherwise people would be overwhelmed by the vast number of events that surrounds them. Daft and Weick (2001, 242) assert how the interpretation in the organizations is the process of translating events, developing sensemaking models and connecting the conceptual schemas. This perspective means that people act in the ways that confirm their propositions about the external world. That way the socially constructed world imposes limits to orientation and action. Related routines and usual patterns of activity are such socially constructed way of adjustment of interpretations. In a somewhat different context, the same argument is made by Antoine de Saint Exupery (1943, 45–46):

> The next day the little prince came back. "It would have been better to come back at the same hour," said the fox. "If, for example, you come at four o'clock in the afternoon, then at three o'clock I shall begin to be happy. I shall feel happier and happier as the hour advances. At four o'clock, I shall already be worrying and jumping about. I shall show you how happy I am! But if you come at just any time, I shall never know at what hour my heart is to be ready to greet you... One must observe the proper rites."

Besides the potential conflict of interpretations between organizational agents, the complexity of organizational dynamics is also influenced by the tensions between individual interpretations and something we can call an "organizational mind"—a kind of amalgam of mechanistic and rational interest of entities that hold positions of power. An organizational mind is evident in a coherent and meaningful set of rules set by the management. Thinking patterns of organization members are influenced by these rules, but not entirely. Simon (1997, 111) asserts that the cross-section of the two concepts creates an area in which the behavior of the members of the organization is expected and approved. According to Spender (1998, 14), the existence of these tensions is the very reason management research is required.

The existence of an organizational mind suggests that the idea of cognition can be applied in organizations in a similar manner as applied to individuals. By adopting this assumption we rise above the limited scope of mechanistic or "objective" principles of classical management theory. The difference between individual and organizational cognition can be found in the fact that in the case of individual cognition there is a certain level of awareness that is innate to human beings. Spender (1998, 29), however, warns that the problem of organizational cognition is not exhausted by the development of a set of organizational roles and rules. It can be done with ease. The problem is to explain the development of a higher level of collective consciousness that is the foundation of autonomous organizational cognition and behavior.

Collective or group "mind" is possible at the level in which the group members share purpose and values. Organizational system of shared values, beliefs and norms are often referred to as the concept of organizational culture. Spender (1998, 17) noticed that the terms "organizational culture" and "collective mind" are difficult to separate, although sometimes used interchangeably.

Enacting organization's environment

Individual interpretations and the resulting activities form and anchor a common understanding of the organization. This combination of interpretation and action, which uphold the fact that people often construct part of the environment they face, Karl Weick (1979) named the "organizational enactment." The enacted perspective of organizational dynamics holds how "[m]anagers construct, rearrange, single out, and demolish many 'objective' features of their surroundings. When people act they randomized variables, insert vestiges of orderliness, and create their constraints" (243). As we will later explore in detail, the organizational enactment is a medium for implementation of radical change.

The importance of the notion of enactment is that it points to the importance of cognitive processes and actions in dealing with the environment. The interpretation has a vital role among the cognitive processes because the interaction of interpretations is what constitutes an organization. The manager's interpretations form the reality he eventually has to cope with. This constructed reality is the principal arena in which all organizational decision making takes place.

Coping with the world, what the management is all about, is more on the action side than on the thinking side. Action constructs the environment people face in the same manner as thinking. The notion of organizational enactment, therefore, includes both—thinking and action. Once the managers conceive the decision making situation in their minds, they start acting as if the situation is reality, and in the process they create contours of the environment or simulate it in order to find meaning in their activities. The process creates a number of if-then relationships in which the activities are related to the results, which subsequently serve as a set of expectations about the future turn of events.

As we have noted earlier, it is not possible to fully control the environment, but it is also not entirely true that it is necessary to adapt to the environment. Managers and the environment are connected in a more complex way than simple adjustments to each other. Whether the paper sent to the journal will be accepted or not depends on the requirements of the editorial board. If the paper conforms to the standards set by the editors, the chances that the article is accepted for publication are higher. However, if the standardization process if too rigid, the creation of new knowledge will be stifled and the quality of the journal will stagnate.

The process of genesis of organizational enactment allows us to understand the dynamics of action constrains by social constructions. Weick (2001a, 182–187) describes the creation of organizational enactment through a two-stage process. The first step is to set aside one section of the flow of experience and submit it to a thorough analysis on the basis of existing concepts. The second step is that the organizational agents than act within the context of the extracted section of experience. It is through the process of creation of enactment that the organizational coherence is defined. It is achieved by the rhetorical action of members of the organization. Through the convergence of the managers' interpretation of the situation (perhaps through discussion) their "realities" are changing, in other words, some external order is imposed. Weick (2001a, 176–177) strongly argues that the process of enactment is generated because of the need of the individuals to identify an external reality in their social relations. Members of organizations think and act in a way that confirms their assumptions. In that way, socially created world becomes a world that constrains the action and thinking.

The cognitive and behavioral relationships that form the organization as well as the causal maps of individual organizational agents are inspired and developed through experience. By showing how presumptions can shape the environment, the concept of enactment allows one to argue the importance of mental schema in the organizational dynamics. The point will be one of the key focuses of the next chapter.

Organizational complexity stems from the fact that each pivotal element of the relationship of interdependence between the two sides is open to creation, negotiation, manipulation, redefinitions and social constructions. In other words, everybody can make a difference. Members of the organization, however, have a different impact on the process of enacting an organization. The strength of interpretation of each member of the organization depends on the intra-organizational political position that depends on both formal and informal factors. The effect of each member of the organizations on the implementation of decisions is denoted by the concept of power (Salancik and Cooper Brindle 1997, 115–116). Power is the potential ability to influence. Social power is the ability to have an effect on other people. Organizational power is the ability to influence the collective organized structure and those who constitute them.

A theory based on the dependence of one organization agent on another is the classical approach to the rationalization of phenomenon of power in social systems (Emerson 1962; Salancik 1977). Every member of an organization involved in the decision making situation will shape his interpretations in respect to his interests. Vectors of dependence on others are one of the most important influences in the process. Decisions, therefore, reflect the dominant dependences in the organization, or in other words the organizational power structure. As a consequence, each individual or shared result in achieving the organization's goal is filtered through the organizational interpretation system (Daft and Weick 1984; Daft and Macintosh 1981). Perceptions of top management or the dominant coalition in position of control will define the final interpretation of the situation. Such interpretation will be the foundation for the development of organizational enactment.

Strategizing as the process of enactment

Organizational enactment should be constructed in a way to correspond with efficient and effective ways of achieving organizational purpose. In that way, strategy can be seen as an interpretive activity pointing to the action that consequently brings cues in the interpretation agenda and enacts socially acceptable behavior.

Since organization agents actively enact the environment through their social interaction, strategy is understood as a result of the process that serves as a tool for bridging the gap between what an organization is now and where we want it to be in the future. In other words, strategy as a way of achieving purpose of the organization is the path through which an organization develops. As Smircich and Stubbard (1985, 724) argue: "The task of strategic management in this view is organization making—to create and maintain the system of shared meaning that facilitates organized action." The radical change is *par excellence* example of strategizing as organizational making.

Term strategy in business organization context bears ambiguous meanings (Mintzberg, Ahlstrand and Lampel 1998). As the structure of changing meanings, strategy's implications and content depend on the context in which they are administered. As a socially constructed reality, strategy exists as a concept as well as a practice, woven into the world and language of managers and organizations. The two dimensions of strategizing are crucial to the perspective of socially constructed organizations—action and thinking. Action can be viewed through the perspective of its key drivers. The question is whether the strategy emerges as a result of managerial discretion—a conscious effort of calculated planning processes undertaken by a team of top managers—or if it is primarily a result of the continuing organizational adjustment and if it, only to the minimal extent, depends on the design of a small group of leading people. On the other hand, the strategy as the thinking process is mainly reflected in the question of whether it is fundamentally a creative or an analytical process. Tipuric (2014, 63–64) depicts these two opposites as key tensions that form responses to the questions of an organization's self-determination, competitiveness and survival (see Figure 2.1). These two dimensions define the framework within which we look at the radical change from strategic management perspective.

The fundamental question that the book aims to answer, concerning the radical change in industrial context, is how the leader can generate and introduce disruption within the enacted environment of an industry that would drive the organization to the position of competitive advantage.

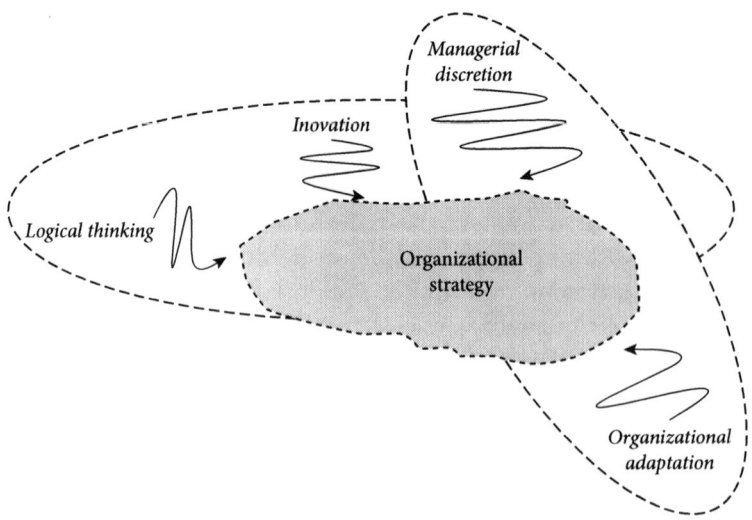

FIGURE 2.1   *Strategic tensions*

Just as a group of people who we define as an organization is, in fact, the process of organizing, we can say that a group of competitors are in the process of strategizing. Drawing on the idea of enactment, Porac, Thomas and Baden-Fuller (1989, 398) coined the term "competitive enactment" which shows functioning of interrelated processes of social construction in the arena of the industry. Just as members of an organization share common conceptions of their environment, so the industry members share a common view on competitive dynamics. An example of an enactment on an inter-organizational level of analysis that Porac, Thomas and Baden-Fuller depict is the case of the community of cashmere wool, the knitwear manufacturer in Hawick, Scotland (398–399). The community of craftsmen from Hawick and the surrounding area jointly construct one another through the choice of materials and production techniques which include questions such as which products should be produced, from where the raw materials are purchased, how to attract customers and the like. Such activities create the distinctive characters of the total market, which are not merely a response to a pre-given environment. Perception of the distinct element directs the development of community's mental model and the subsequent strategic choices. Praised differently, community members use activities to reinforce their identity. Although individual's mental models of competition within a given industry are peculiar at first, they eventually converge through the process of enactment.

Change as a process of sensemaking

Radical decision leads to radical change. Managing processes of change is one of the key themes in business administration literature. The word "change" has several contradictory meanings. Sometimes it refers to the external changes, especially in the technology but also in the competitive dynamics, consumer demands, political environment and the like. Also, the term "change" may relate to the elements within the organizational system. Regardless of the vector from which they originate, the fundamental goal of change management is to align internal and external dynamics.

The study of organizational change is an area which offers great possibilities for the concepts of managerial cognition (Gioia 1986; Weick and Bougon 1986; Gioia and Chittipeddi 1991). Within the paradigm of managerial and organizational cognition, the change management is defined as a process of dealing with the ways of how individuals cope and interact in novel situations. For the purpose of explaining the phenomena of radical decision making, the definition of organizational change is set in the theoretical framework which views organizational life as an ongoing experience of thinking and acting. According to Weick (1979, 188–193), organizations are in the process of organizing, and therefore they undergo constant change. In the organizational dynamics change occurs because of the process of reacting to novel situations. For the purpose of explaining how people react to novel situations, we will explore the theoretical framework of "sensemaking" (Weick 1995; Brown 2000), the concept which will be used as the cornerstone of the radical decision making process.

The phenomenon of search for meaning is ubiquitous. Sensemaking, as Weick (1995, 109–111) explains, begins with three elements: the frame, the element taken out of the flow of experience and the bond between them. The meaning is formed from the cue within the concrete frame in which members of the organization locate, perceive and identify events. Cues are noticed and made meaningful within the frames. Frames are, usually, previous moments of socialization, and the cues are, usually, present elements of experience. The search for meaning is based on finding the cue, a metaphor that leads us to the construction of an "oasis" of sense out of otherwise meaningless elements that constitute the current state of affairs. The desire to make sense of the situations steams from the need to safeguard the conception of the existence of the world that is stable. A stable world is characterized by pre-given qualities where all information is readily available. By giving up the idea of the world as a fixed and stable reference point, we fall into idealism, nihilism or subjectivism, which is not something everybody likes. The alternative, according to Beck, Brüderl and Woywode (2008), is to accept that the groundlessness of the interaction is the foremost feature of the rich textures of the interdependent world of social relations.

The search for meaning in everyday life is not identical to the same process in organizations. The principal difference is that organizations are social constructions that significantly influence the formation of meaning. According to Giddens (1976, 7), social structures are created in the process of establishment of meaning, and at the same time they bound it. Organizational context is also specific from the perspective of existence of multiple meanings of activities in the process of sensemaking, an issue that will prove to be very relevant in the implementation part of radical decision making. Gergen (1982, 62–65) highlights the role of activity in three premises of sensemaking. Firstly, identification of any action is subject to constant revision. The reason for this is that organizational life takes place in a dynamic context which also changes the meaning of earlier events. Secondly, the foundation of any identification is based on networks of interdependent and changing interpretations. Meaning of action is rarely self-evident. Since the identification is determined by the specific context and since the context is continually expanding in the future and the past, it is not clear what contextual indicators in the process of searching for meaning can be taken as reliable. The opposing groups will want to emphasize the importance of the events that are more appropriate for their goals. Thirdly, any activity is subject to the multiple identifications whose comparative advantage is questionable. To call something a "problem" is no better or more sustainable than to call the same event an "opportunity." What is interesting is that one and the other proposal may initiate a series of activities that will validate the selected stand.

From the broadest perspective, sensemaking is a metaphor that draws attention to the idea that reality must be seen as an ongoing activity, which takes shape when individuals attempt to bring order and retrospectively make sense of the situation in which they find themselves (Morgan, Frost and Pondy 1983; Morgan 1980). Once we find the meaning, we can provide it to the others. That is the process of leadership.

Leading as the process of sensegiving

Although literature is rife with description of leadership functions, leaders basically do two things—articulate the goals of the organization and strategies for achieving these goals and motivate organizational agents to carry out strategies. Leaders who are good at setting strategies and motivating will make the organization more effective, and who are less good at performing these jobs will pull the organization down. In a nutshell—leaders make their organizations what they are. In a *Fortune* interview, published in the last December issue of 2011, as an answer to the question of what his greatest creation is, iPhone or iPad, Steve Jobs said: "Apple—the company. Because anybody can create products, but Apple keeps creating great products." Leadership in complex organizations recognizes that the future cannot be controlled (in a deterministic sense) because complex systems are unpredictable and future conditions are determined by the internal dynamics. Leaders have to think systemically and to stay aware of the interactive dynamics since they are one element of an interactive network we call "organization." The role of the leader is not to control the networks because it cannot be done but to help enable useful behaviors, including the expansion and complexification of the networks. Therefore, the complexity theory suggests that leadership should not concentrate on organizational control but rather on supporting the capacity of the organization.

If we think the organizations as made of entities based on multiple interpretations of interactions which consequently create the enactment of the social systems, we will eventually have to find an answer to the fundamental question of organizing: how to coordinate actions in a world of multiple realities? A possible answer to this question is the observation of the organization as a social form that generates a unique understanding which can be replicated by the people who were not involved in the original construction. Managing the transition from the individual relationship to a more general comparison is to manage the tensions that arise when people try to reconcile innovation, inherent in a personal relationship, with a control derived from the generic subjectivity. Reconciliation of these two poles of organizational interaction is achieved by intertwined routines and usual patterns of behavior, both of which have their origin in individual interactions. Forms of social organization, in principle, consist of activities based on a formula that is developed and maintained through continuous communication activity. As Weick (1995, 117) asserts, the key communication goal is to develop a common understanding of the decision making situation.

The leadership process is defined through the alignment of interpretations and actions of organizational members. Conveying meaning is known in the literature as the process of "sensegiving" (Gioia and Chittipeddi 1991; Hill and Levenhagen 1995).

Sensegiving can be defined as the process by which the leader is trying to influence the sensemaking of the organization members in order to uphold the preferred redefinition of organizational reality (Hodgkinson and Sparrow 2002, 25–26). The sensegiving model as a sequential process was first introduced by Gioia and Chittipeddi (1991). According to the model, the leader, firstly, establishes a mental representation of his initial search for meaning, and, secondly, communicates it to the members of the organization who build their sense of it. Realization of leader's mental representation demands action which is based on the sense created by the activities of organizational members. The action can be viewed as a feedback on the results of the leader's sensemaking process. In return, through the interaction with other interpretations, the leader's initial representation changes again. That circular process of sensemaking and "sensewitnessing" is one of the key organizational activities in coping with change. Since cognitive competencies result with behavioral competencies, the sensemaking and sensegiving processes are crucial for the success of top management in the process of radical change.

The decision maker provides meaning to the members of the organization through the set of political skills. Hodkingson and Sparrow (2002, 238–239) emphasize that major decisions are basically procedures of simplification that are used for the purpose of highlighting the appropriate balance in terms of the level of complexity. The notion is relevant for radical decision making because in this kind of situation the leader must use clear, simple and action-oriented messages in order to connect the desired future state with current preoccupations. Only in this way can the leader maintain "zones of relative control" which would allow stability, crucially needed for launching of new ideas.

In the interest of avoiding the divergence of the interpretations of the situation between the organizational agents, in other to be able to make effective decisions, the leader must find a way of focusing the process of interpretation. Otherwise, members of the organization will be overwhelmed and preoccupied with differing interpretations of their past activities. Weick (2001d, 13–14) argues that a powerful mechanism for routing of interpretations can be a process of behavioral commitment. Binding behavior focuses process of searching for meaning on three things: activity, socially acceptable justifications and additional activities to confirm the justification. In that way the sensegiving process is conducted indirectly, through commitment to action. The use of action as a rhetorical tool in radical decision making is described in detail in the last chapter of the book.

3
Building Mental Models for Effective Leadership

Abstract: *Opening with an engaging narrative about famous inventor Nikola Tesla, Hruška sets the reader into the information processing paradigm. Two research paradigms, paramount for the depiction of radical decision making, the managerial and organizational cognition and the personal development theory, are explored. The author also describes elements of human cognitive apparatus, which are of essential use in organizational psychology: perception, mental models construction, adaptive learning and action. Finally, Hruška elaborates on how leaders develop competence by reflecting on their experience. The central proposition is how an attribute of experienced professionals in any profession is the development of mental representations that control and sensitize their perception so that they are able to notice the elements of crucial importance for the decision-making situation.*

Keywords: adaptive learning and action; managerial and organizational cognition; mental models construction; perception; personal development theory; reflection

Hruška, Domagoj. *Radical Decision Making: Leading Strategic Change in Complex Organizations.*
New York: Palgrave Macmillan, 2015.
DOI: 10.1057/9781137492319.0007.

The miracle mind

Nikola Tesla is to electricity what Mozart is to music—unquestionably one of the world's greatest geniuses. He was born in 1856 in Smiljani, Croatia. In 1884, he went to the United States where he stayed until his death in 1943. He was an inventor of new devices but was much more than that. Tesla was the discoverer of new principles, opening many new areas of knowledge that even today have been only partly explored. Tesla's principal contribution to the field of electromagnetic engineering is the invention of the rotating magnetic field and the polyphase electrical system. He also conducted pioneering experiments in fluorescent lighting, vacuum tube, radio, robotics and X-ray technologies (O'Neill 1996, 28). Tesla's discovery of the rotating magnetic field, as well as his inventions of the transformer and induction motor, was valuable advancements that are still in use today. His best-known invention, alternating current induction motor, made the universal transmission and distribution of electrical energy possible and spurred on the development of the modern age.

Tesla had by all accounts a flawless photographic memory but more important is that he had a unique method of discovering new truths through the unique mental processes of visualizing constructs long before they were actually produced. This unusual proficiency in use of mental models helped his work in a way that he spent much less time and money than by using the usual trial-and-error approach. He could build a mental model of the engine, take it apart piece by piece and put it back together again. Tesla built prototype machines entirely in his mind and then dictated the dimensions of the pieces to the machinists who cut the metal. The pieces fit together perfectly, and he never had to adjust any of them. Tesla (2007a, 19) highlights this issue in his autobiography: "When I get an idea I start at once building it up in my imagination. I change the construction, make improvements and operate the device in my mind. It is immaterial to me whether I run my turbine in my thought or test it in my shop. I even note if it is out of balance."

Although Tesla's ability to construct mental models was remarkable, we have to bear in mind that the problems he was dealing with are of positivistic nature, without uncertainty and ambiguity that define mental models of organizational dynamics. This point is noted by Tesla as well (2007a, 20):

> Invariably my device works as I conceived that it should, and the experiment comes out exactly as I planned it. In twenty years, there has not been a single exception. Why should it be otherwise? Engineering, electrical and

mechanical, is positive in results. There is scarcely a subject that cannot be mathematically treated and the effects calculated or the results determined beforehand from the available theoretical and practical data.

Tesla's ability to construct and work with mental models with this kind of accuracy shows that building and refining mental models of decision making situation is an activity worth every effort. Even with the blurriness that always accompanies the presence of human factor, the radical decision maker wants to learn to master the use of mental models. Only by realizing the current situation and by visualizing the future state can we implement radical change.

Managerial and organizational cognition

The term "cognition" refers to how people collect, modify and interpret information from the surroundings or the information already stored in their minds, and how they retrieve them in order to created knowledge (Neisser 1976). Cognition examines various processes associated with making sense of the situation such as categorization, usage of the structure of knowledge (cognitive schemas) and development of mental models (scenarios) (van der Heijden 2005; Spender 1998). Therefore, all activities that we use to understand the world and act accordingly are a matter of cognition. In order to understand how a leader who wants to enact radical change creates understanding of the environment that he is facing, we need to comprehend a set of well-founded knowledge about human cognition.

Modern cognitive science can be traced back to the Descartes analysis of our "impression" of reality. Descartes (1984, 21) draws attention to the ways in which wax makes an impression on a seal and claims that this is similar to the imprinting of sensory impressions on the surface of our minds. Today, however, we know that mental models are not direct impressions of the reality on the clean surface of our consciousness. They are the result of the complex process of sorting, manipulation and conversion that are shaped by our present knowledge, intentions and interests. Application of the theoretical frameworks from the area of cognition in the study of organizations is a propulsive research field. The model of implementing radical change is embedded in the research paradigm of managerial and organizational cognition. Research framework of managerial and organizational cognition analyzes subsystems of higher mental processes and their role in decision-making (Eden, Jones and Sims 1979; Eden and Spender 1998; Lachman, Lachman and Butterfield 1979). The area of study fully formed in the past 20 years, but its beginnings can be set in the time of development of information processing paradigm in psychology research. In the late 1950s of the past century occurred a change of paradigm in a number of scientific fields now known as a "cognitive revolution." Herbert Simon, George Miller and Noam Chomsky are the forerunners of a new research paradigm of human nature. Their interest was not in analyzing the objective reactions of respondents to the stimulus as it was in the dominant psychology paradigm before them. They wanted to discover what the respondents know, how they learn and how the knowledge is used. The research emphasis has, therefore, shifted from what people are doing to what people know.

In the debate on the foundations of cognitive science, Simon and Kaplan (1989) report that cognitive science is based on three approaches of studying intelligence and intelligent process: in the abstract sense, in computer research and in the analysis of human thinking. From this point of view, we need to develop models of the human mind as well as the knowledge that is processed in such mental models. We also need to understand the relationship among the content, the modeled process (between knowledge and choices) and human behavior.

In respect to organizational dynamics, the main objectives of cognitive paradigm are to define ways in which people in organizations define the situation, become aware of alternative courses of action, evaluate the consequences of these actions and consider the significance of the action in a socially constructed world (Eden Jones, and Sims 1979, 4). The scientific approach to these questions through the research paradigm of managerial and organizational cognition is focused on the development of models and knowledge structures as well as on their implications for the organizational context.

Theories of rational expectations and managerial choices, which continue to dominate the curriculum of business schools through the world, provide a very specific view of managerial cognition and organizational rationality. Paradigm of managerial and organizational cognition in principle rejects the assumption that managerial decision-making can be adequately analyzed through rational assumption of complete data, well-defined objective function and the rigorous logic of the selection process.

Although the application of cognitive theory to the study of organizations is a relatively new phenomenon, the need for cognitive approach to managerial and organizational analysis can be found in many "classics" of organizational theory and the theory of strategy. Thus, Weick (1995, 66) notes that Barnard's (1938) text on the functions of the executive introduced the idea of the organizations as systems of action, consciously coordinated through the controlled information processing and communication. Simon (1997), on the other hand, lays the foundations of modern cognitive theories in organizational studies by introducing the idea that decisions are never entirely rational due to limitations in the capabilities of information processing. Furthermore, March and Simon (1993) emphasize the cognitive dimension of managerial work through the elaboration of the ways in which organizational routines release the attention that can be put in use for the non-routine decision making. Although the foundations of application of the cognitive perspective in management can be found in these and other classic works, it is only in the past 15–20 years that the discipline of organizational and managerial cognition has grown into a separate research area.

The need to focus on the cognitive paradigm of organizational behavior has led to the development of the set of theories within the area of naturalistic decision making. Naturalistic models emphasize cognitive processes associated with creating images on the situation, mainly through categorization (Mervis and Rosch 1981; Klein 2008), the use of knowledge structures (cognitive schemas) (Ackerman and Eden 2011) and the construction of mental models (scenarios) (Lipshitz 1989; van der Heijden 2005). Approach to decision making from the perspective of managerial and organizational cognition differs from the previous approaches precisely in the fact that it focuses on real managerial action, not the abstract rational models. For instance, the concept that has played a major role in research of individual and organizational decision making is the concept of bounded rationality (Simon 1997, 118–122). Namely, the idea that managers make decisions in a situation of complete information, well-defined and logical information process is not consistent with the reality of organizational life. Managers do not have complete information, knowledge or the competence to process a large amount of available information (March and Simon 1993, 157–193).

Proponents of managerial and organizational cognition hold that managers form personal models of decision making situations and that these models significantly differ from the abstract models that are presumed by the formal theory of choice. Thus, one of the ways that we can define the area of managerial and organizational cognition is the nature and the origin of the difference between the models of the "real manager" and abstract, rational models of utility theory. According to Spender and Eden (1998, 3-4), instead of looking at the manager from the perspective of the computer processor, the cognition view takes him as a key subject in the creation of limited strategic space that forms the basis for the selection process. According to this view, we are unable to predict the nature of managerial response a priori. On the other hand, we assume that we can gain insight into personal models that managers make and use in the decision making. Major areas of interest are the limits and structures of these constructed models as well as the methods of their use. These questions are focusing the research areas of managerial and organizational cognition toward the area of cognitive, not behavioral sciences (e.g., as the field of behavioral economics). These restrictions affect the fact that in the research of radical decision making we are primarily concerned with the process and not so much on the results of the decision.

The four basic principles of decision making research from the perspective of managerial and organizational cognition set by Hodgkinson and Sparrow (2002, 11), also apply to the mental processes of changing organizational paradigm that is the focus of radical decision making. First principle is that individuals are limited in processing large number of different and complex stimuli from the environment. Second, they use a variety of strategies aimed at relieving the burdens of information processing. Third, the individuals develop a simplified understanding of reality that is stored in their minds. Finally, mental representations serve as filters through which the upcoming information is progressively processed. Special focus of radical change phenomena is on the third and consequently the fourth of these principles—the question of how leaders construct mental models that govern their thinking and action.

The constructivist paradigm of human understanding

The constructivist paradigm of human understanding deals with the ways through which people make sense of the situation and act according to it. The key perspective that personal construction theory offers to the implementation of radical decisions is that people do not work in some kind of primal reality, independent of our mind and the minds of those around them.

Constructivist paradigm is set forward by the personal construction theory introduced by George Kelly (1955). The constructivist viewpoint is at the same time the philosophy of science, art and knowledge. The central thesis of constructivism is that contrary to the common sense there is no single reality which is independent of human mental activity and human symbolic language. In other words, what we call the world is the product of our mind, within which we construct the world by the symbolic processes. This leads us to the conclusion that one's world is no realer than others, none of the mental representations of the world, no one's truth, is ontologically more correct than the other. Personal constructions of reality are particularly important in the social sciences; such is the organizational theory, where reference framework has the largest influence on what we see, how we explain it and how it directs our activities.

The process of personal construction of reality starts with the perception that continues with the construction of mental models, but its real importance is gained through interpretation. As discussed in the last chapter, interpretation can be described as a form of explanation that requires a particular understanding or knowledge. In some forms of the functioning of the mind, such as perception, it is quite evident that a large part of what we distinguish is a constructivist process. What we perceive is very directly affected by our expectations, desires and a number of other similar influences.

Most of the things we know about the elements of organizational choice as well as about their probable consequences are reflected in our interpretation, which is also a constructivist process. Daft and Weick (1984) "interpret the interpretation" as a means of decoding external events to internal categories that are part of the culture of the community that the decision maker belongs to. The act of interpretation involves creating mental representations that simplify certain territory in the interest of facilitating action. Different interpretations of the same situation lead us to the conclusion that there is never only one possible explanation of the decision making situation. Each formed interpretation is in principle a special world, constructed by the individual.

The constructivist nature of human understanding is perhaps best seen through the idea of constructive memory. Contrary to the common opinion memory is not like a large library in which we store recollections and knowledge. Memory has a constructive character. Among others, support to the constructivist theories of the nature of memory was given by Sigmund Freud (1911, chap. 1, doc. B) in his descriptions of how people falsify and re-model their experiences.

Frederic Charles Bartlett (2010) introduced the idea of the constructivist nature of memory while particularly significant contribution to the idea was specified by Ulrich Neisser (1976, 75). Neisser claimed that remembering is like problem solving—existing knowledge and memory of previous reconstructions is used to create the possible interpretations of the past event. The idea that the remembering is reconstruction suggests that we reconstruct memory of the past but with the influence of our current beliefs. Hence the idea that people's beliefs remained relatively stable over time (Ross 1989). Continuity of identity derived from the reconstructive nature of memory affects the reluctance of accepting changes and encourages the acceptance of the *status quo*. A radical decision implies deliberate breaking of inadequate and stale value structures.

The constructivist paradigm states that remembering and construction of mental models depends on what we have observed, the information that we have previously collected and schematic modifications that have occurred. We cannot recall what we did not perceive, and we cannot see the modified schemata if it is not used. Constructivist perspective on functioning of human cognitive apparatus centers our attention on the process of perception.

Perception is reality

Perception and cognition are not only operations in the mind, but also the transactions with the world. These transactions not only inform the observer, but they also change him. What we perceive is the result of communication between past experiences, which include cultural influences and interpretations of what is perceived. If the object of perception is not supported by these perceptual foundations, it is likely that it will not exceed the perceptual threshold. Neisser (1976, 20–21) notes that, in principle, the process of perception is always changing what we see. When we see something with a preconceived idea of what an object of observation represents, we have a tendency to compare the perceived reality with the existing ideas. The problem stems from the fact that people are unable to understand new information if they do not depend on their existing knowledge. When an object is observed without understanding, in an attempt to understand what it is about, the mind will try to reach for something that it already recognizes— something that we have experienced and what resembles the most to the unknown object.

So, we only perceive objects that we can recognize or that fits an existing conceptual structure that "makes sense." One of the features that characterize experienced decision makers is the presence of conceptual structures that control and direct perception. Such decision makers notice important things that others might miss.

In addition to its constructivist nature, perception is also an active process. To a large extent we choose what we see, we select certain objects in the range of our attention and ignore others. The concept of perception, in its broad sense, refers to the entire process of understanding of objects and events from the environment—their observation, understanding, identification, labeling and preparation of response to them. The process of perception can be best understood if we split it into two phases: observation and recognition of the environmental stimuli.

Observation is the conversion of physical energy collected by the sensory system in the neural codes recognized by the brain. The sensing system is a system composed of several senses of the body, which collect different types of sensory neurons: sight, hearing, touch, smell and taste. Certain sensory stimuli enter our mind, while others do not. The mechanism that regulates the selection of sensory stimuli is called attention. Attention is willing mental focus on the selected number of relevant elements that have a central importance in our awareness. At the same time, we ignore the multitude of other stimuli. Attention is directed by our personal goals and the characteristics of the objects. Given the great importance of the concept of attention for radical decision making, the process of attention will be elaborated in more details in the exploration of the genesis of governing mental representation of radical mental model.

It is one thing to be aware of stimuli in the surroundings, and quite another to become fully consciously aware of what we have perceived. Our perceptual system not only captures information about the world, but it also actively categories and interprets them. Identification and recognition add meaning to the observed objects. The answer that we want to give at this stage of the perception process is what the observed object really is and not only how it looks like, which was the focus of the observation phase.

Identification and recognition of the objects as well as the identification of best possible reaction to it involves high-level cognitive processes such as theories of action, values, beliefs and attitudes concerning the object. In order to devise actions in response to the recognized stimuli, we have to build complex mental structures—mental models.

The cognitive problem solving apparatus

While it is possible to perceive a given situation in numerous ways, it is always structured of the same elements. These elements include language, behavior, images and the like. The fundamental concepts of human understanding are called mental schemata. The concepts are applied to a specific situation and form "ideas" or mental models.

The process of mental model construction starts from the already elaborated premise of "perceived reality." Through the process of perception, to a certain extent, people choose what they see. They select certain objects to focus attention on while the others are ignored. Perception is directed by the existing mental structures or mental schemes. When a problem occurs, collection of anticipatory schemes is formed from the existing schemes that are stored in the long-term memory (resulting from previous perceptual experiences). The selective nature of perception and the process of retrieval of existing schemes allow the leaders to construct simplified mental conceptualizations of decision-making situations called the mental representations (Rumelhart and Norman 1988). Specific kind of mental representations—that expresses overall representation of the surroundings—the relationships between its various parts and a person's intuitive perception about her own acts and their consequences are called mental maps (Tolman 1948) or mental models (Johnson-Laird 2010, 1983).

From the perspective of radical decision making, mental schemata and mental models play a key role in the decision making process. Through the process of construction and crystallization of mental models the decision maker reduces the complexity associated with the business environment and, in that process, determines which stimuli from the environment will be observed and which will be ignored (Starbuck and Milliken 1988, 51). Cognitive view on decision making assumes that a leader builds models of the decision making situation in his mind and that these models help him to find meaning that consequently directs his action.

First we will explore the role of mental schemes. Reading, listening, observing and dealing with reality at every level depend on existing cognitive structures—mental schemes. The concept of mental schemes comes from the British cognitive psychologist Bartlett (2010), who defined the concept as an active organization of past reactions or past experiences. Mental schemes are structures that represent certain aspects of the world. They are impartial units that carry meaning. The scheme can be a causal relationship, the single element of experience as well as a complex set of elements. The thread of coherence between the elements is what makes an amalgam of experience a mental scheme.

People use schemes to organize existing knowledge and provide frameworks for future understanding of the world such as stereotypes, social roles, archetypes and the like. Through the use of schemes, most everyday situations do not require intensive thinking. Mental activity, therefore, can be reduced almost to the level of automation. People can organize new objects of perception in the mental schemes and can operate them effectively without much effort. For example, most people have in mind the mental scheme of the stairs and are, therefore, perfectly able to climb the stairs that were never climbed before. Each person has unique capabilities of perception and action, because no one occupies the same position in the world, and no one has the same history. With regard to the organizational processes that we deal with, it is particularly important to emphasize that Neisser (1976, 54–56) argued how mental schemes go through the process of accommodation. In the course of this process, the decision maker becomes what he is through what he had perceived and done in the past.

Mental schemes influence our perception, memory and behavior in the most profound way. Bartlett (2010, chap. 10, section 2) described memory as a creative process of reconstruction of such schemes. According to the theory of mental schemes, perception, understanding, interpretation and memory are based on these structures of knowledge organization. The importance of expectations in the search for meaning in a new experience is well known. The mental schemes incorporate these expectations. In the case of reading, for example, schemes provide mental frameworks that help the reader to understand what they read (Bruner 1990, 61–63). As we mentioned in the discussion on the nature of perception, information can be collected only if there are already developed formats that can accept them and the information that does not fit these formats are not used. In other words, mental schemes act as filters—they keep put the information that is not in accordance with them. The impact of mental schemes to remembering is characterized by the fact that we only remember information that is consistent with our existing schemes. One interesting consequence of this phenomenon is known as a self-fulfilling prophecy (Snyder 1984, 254). According to this mental process, our mental schemes become reality because of our unconscious behavior toward others that are conducted in a way that leads them to behave in accordance with our schemes.

Hodgkinson and Sparrow (2002, 21–22) expound that mental schemes can be extremely useful if properly organized. Proper organization of mental schemes implies high-quality information and dense and sophisticated links between interconnected structures. If these kind of schemes exits, the manager is able to understand the events of the environment, can decode and effectively pull the information for flow of experience, can work out more convenient and more accurate interpretations and resolve problems faster. However, too much reliance on such knowledge structures can result in many negative connotations and can restrict manager's understanding of the environment. Potential hazards include a stereotypical way of thinking, uncontrolled processing of information, incorrect data filtering and rejection of unusual, but important information or overall inhibition toward solving problems. These dangers are particularly pronounced in the case of radical decision making.

Like other schemes, mental models accept information and direct action. As I have a scheme of the pencil on my desk which accepts the information about the pencil and directs further investigation, I also have cognitive maps of the entire table, which allows me to receive information about the desk and direct my orientation, including the process of finding the pen. Mental scheme of the pen is part of a wider orientation scheme—mental model of the table. The term "cognitive map" is interesting because it highlights the fact that the search for meaning is similar to the process of mapping a given area. The geographical map entirely embodies in itself a set of rules for finding one's way through a region of otherwise uncharted experiences. What is found on the map depends on what the cartographer is looking at, how he is looking as well as which tools he is using. The key thing in cartography is that there is no "one best map" for a particular turf. As Weick (2001b, 8–9) points out, for every area there is an infinitely large number of useful maps, arising from the large number of descriptions of the terrain, models of display and possibilities of usage. The task of the decision maker is not to search for an exact image that corresponds to the current reality. The problem is that the field is constantly changing, and the task of the decision maker is to find an area of stability in a constant flow of changes that will allow him to make a decision. When we say that an organization or a part of it and the associated environment is in the mind of the decision maker, we think of two things. First, such a causal map affects the construction of a new experience through the mechanisms of expectations, and second, the causal maps influence the interpretation of past experience through the mechanism of highlighting the appropriate elements in the current organizational context. We can say that by the use of mental models we rely on theoretical guidance for the interpretation of our experience and in the same way reduce the importance of our impressions to what they are—an uncertain and probably deceptive expressions of reality.

The reason to begin with the construction of mental models is the need to cope with the problem situation. When confronted with a problem situation, the decision maker must agree on what the problem is, fully understand it and find a way of stating the problem to himself (build a mental representation) before he starts looking for a solution (Simon 1977, 74). Problems in business do not just present themselves to the decision maker, but they need to be constructed from a material of the problem situation which is always confusing, uncertain and complicated. Problems are constructions of the mind, always consisting of several well-known and several unfamiliar terms. Problem solving is more a kind of a wrestling activity than it is about getting to know the various doctrines (Polanyi 1957, 90–91). Problem areas in business administration are never connected only to one discipline. They are transdisciplinary. If you want to find and solve a business problem, you do not need to know all mental schemes from the different disciplines, but just few concepts relevant for the problem in hand and their relationships. In a so-called lost interview broadcasted on May 14, 1990, by the WGBH, Apple's Steve Jobs puts forward the same point of leader's transdisciplinary: "Leonardo was the artist but he also mixed all his own paints. He also was a fairly good chemist. He knew about pigments, knew about human anatomy. And combining all of those skills together, the art and the science, the thinking and the doing, was what resulted in the exceptional result. And there is no difference in our industry." As Baracskai, Dörfler and Velencei

(2005, 50–51) stress, putting down deep roots in only one discipline and avoidance of exploration of the unknown inevitably leads to relaxation and stagnation.

When we are setting the problem or in other words when we are searching for meaning in a problem situation, we are actually setting the boundaries of our attention in a way that allows us to say what is wrong and in which direction the situation needs to be changed. Setting the problem is a process in which, interactively, we choose the things to pay attention to and hence provide the context within which we will cultivate the chosen concepts (Schön 1991, 40). Previous decisions set the framework of attention that mind utilizes in the specific decision making situation. Simon (1997, 108–109) points out that this narrow frame of focus is substantially different from the broad scope of attention that we have used when we first were introduced to this kind of decision making situation.

Refining mental models through adaptive learning

Due to his limited cognitive capabilities, the decision maker resorts to the use of mental models, which represent reduced versions of real world dynamics. As argued earlier, the human cognitive apparatus is inherently subjective. Reason for subjectivity of perception is limited information processing capacity. The limited cognitive capacity is also the most significant reason for the complexity of the world around us. If the limitation of conscious thinking is a fundamental obstacle to understanding the world, the question is which methods are available to improve decision-making? According to Eden, Jones and Sims (1979, 27–31), there are two basic ways in which the decision-maker can overcome cognitive limitations. First one is to improve information collection and increase their quality, and second one is to enhance the process of reasoning in the decision making process. The reasoning is the process of upgrading and using mental models.

The usage of mental models is a notoriously challenging activity. Wind, Crook, and Gunther (2005, xxiv) depict the process in this way:

> The first step is to recognize the power and limits of the models. The second step is to test the relevance of the mental models against changing environment and to generate new models. The third step is to overcome inhibitors such as lack of information, lack of trust, desire to hold on to old patterns,

and the expectations of the others. The final step is to implement the model, assess the model and continuously strengthen the model.

Each stage of the process is characterized by uncertainty and ambiguity.

In order to be useful, the initial mental model needs to be improved by adding additional schemata and additional connections between schemata. Mental models are, therefore, constantly updated with new experience and knowledge which is a learning process. Through the learning process, mental models can be refined to better represent real dynamics of decision making situation. Learning about the concepts is about building a set of expectations which enables us to deal with the situation in hand. Language is used to sum up this body of expectations. Learning models are quite important for radical decision making because, as I will discuss in more details in the next chapter, in order to think differently first we need to be good at thinking.

As argued before, the mental models are not direct impressions of reality to the clean the surface of our awareness. They are results of complex processes of sorting, manipulating and converting that shape present knowledge, intentions and interests. The mental models arise from activities and are based on interpretations, continuing active role in the formation of organizational context and the impact of social context on the individual. In a decision making situation, the leader builds a mental model through the collection of specific signals and information with the aim to amend the existing situation. As a first step, the leader builds a mental representation that is based on already collected signals. Such mental representations show the world as a leader "sees" it at that point. The leader then wants to gather as much useful information as possible in order to build a new mental representation. There are two possibilities in respect to clarity of the initial conceptualization of the problem of choice. First, the initial leader's conceptualization of the situation can be characterized low level of uncertainty and ambiguous. In these situations, the leader can quickly and easily decide on what action to take. But the initial conceptualization can also be confusing and incomplete, and the leader will not instantly rely on it while making a decision. In such cases, it is necessary to conduct further research and modifications in the conceptualization of the decision making situation. The second case of mental model evolution is characteristic of the radical decision making process.

To an experienced leader, decision making is a continuous process of reasoning, evaluating the validity and importance of the situation. The process connects decision makers with previous experiences, knowledge, and possible implications. This psychological process does not lead to a situation where it means everything that the decision maker wants it to mean. The mental schemes must be actively used in order to make sense out of the experience. Also, people are using different schemes for handling same experience, and that leads them to different interpretations.

The learning process is a process of interpretation, which Daft and Weick (2001, 244–245) describe through three steps. Each of the steps has its place in the radical decision making process. The first phase of the organizational interpretation is called scanning. Scanning can be defined as monitoring of the environment in order to provision the information for decision making. In the second phase, by use of the mind, meaning is assigned to the collected data. We are going through the process of interpretation when a new construct is introduced to the existing cognitive map. Same happens in organizations. Organizational interpretation is defined as the process of making sense of the events and developing shared understanding and shared conceptual schemes among members of senior management. Interpretation gives meaning to data prior to the organizational learning and activity. Learning is, therefore, the third phase of the process of interpretation. Learning differs from interpretation because it incorporates the concept of action. Based on the interpretation, learning requires a new response or a new activity. Learning is a process of converting a cognitive theory into action (Argyris and Schön 1978; Argyris 1976, 1982). In that way, from the feedback by activities, the act of learning provides new data for interpretation.

Daniel Kahneman (2013, 19–109) points out that we have two different thought processes. One is slow, based on expertise-building that allows us to organize and access a body of evidence about the decision making situation. The other is the quick decision making that we might have to do when we are forced to recognize new patterns or respond to the emotional urges that administer the way we treat people around us. The key to learning is the ability to recognize patterns for what we use anticipatory mental schemata. They prepare us to accept a particular type of information, and not the other, and thus control the activity of observation. Because we only see what we're looking for, it is the scheme, together with the available information, that determines what will be perceived. A set of existing mental scheme prepares the mind to the perception of the elements from the environment and can be viewed as a control structure for the key cognitive processes of perception, attention and categorization. This is where the constructivist nature of perception comes from.

The process of connecting objects or stimuli to categories is called pattern-recognition or stereotyping. The mind, in the process of perception, provides a way in which incoming information is organized. In the process, the mind functions as a self-organizing information system that enables the input experience to be organized in patterns. As soon as the pattern is formed, the mind no longer has to analyze and classify information. It just takes enough information, and the pattern is activated. However, this process is not automatic, as Neisser (1976, 54–56) notes, we will categorize the object or event only if the situation demands it of us. If there is no competitive pattern, everything that even vaguely resembles the established pattern will be considered as such. Once the pattern is formed, all information that is received by this pattern or channel will "flow" through it—always in the same way, enhancing the pattern in the process.

We often hear people saying: "Why do I always go through the same problems and make same mistakes all the time." The answer is—because you are not able to break the patterns of your thinking. But they can be broken. Making radical change happened is about establishing new mental pathways, new frames of pattern recognition. The entire conscious life is based on recognizing patterns and changing old ones with new. Literature, film and other fiction crystallize patterns of experience so that they can be absorbed without living them or without learning it through the slow process of induction. Art can also provide us with a range of experiences that we would otherwise not have had. Reading a good fiction book or watching a good movie is not only matter of relaxation but can be very useful for our business as well.

Thinking in action

Business is about action. It appreciates efficiency more than intellectual games. This is why, in our discussions on decision making, we include both—the choice of direction and the implementation of action. At this point, we will examine the relationship between mental models and actions that result from them.

For decades, the researchers of cognitive phenomena and philosophers of the mind have separated cognition and action, taking the position that the main function of the mind is building of mental representations and performance of cognitive tasks. Rigid distinction between the steps of sensory information processing is a linear three-stage process: perception—cognition—action is, over the last few years, discouraged by many neuropsychological studies that interpret perception and action in terms of their relationship (Giorello and Sinigaglia 2007; Adams and Aizawa 2010).

All of our actions, decisions and plans will be achieved in the future. Therefore, one might think that the action would be obvious and simple after we have collected enough information. But it is not so, the action requires thinking about priorities, consequences and involved people. Not everything is easy once you have accumulated enough information. The skill of action is equally important as the skill of acquiring knowledge. It is especially true in organizational dynamics, since the action is fundamental idiom of business. Apple's Steve Jobs nicely presented the interconnectedness of the two in the already mentioned WGBH interview from 1990:

> My observation is that the doers are the major thinkers. The people that create the things that change this industry are both the thinker and doer in one person...But, usually, when you dig a little deeper, you find that the people that really did it were also the people that really worked through the hard intellectual problems as well.

When a person is active, the environment organizes itself in a cognitive as well as in a physical way. As Weick (2001a, 179) asserts, if we take the view that the reason for the discontinuity of the elements that make up the environment actually is within the organization, and not outside it, the focus of decision-making, of change management and of organizational design should be in the question "What's in there?" And less to the question "What is out there?" Smircich and Stubbard (1985) point out that the idea of an organizational and environmental enactment, and thus the phenomenon of the cognitive approach to decision making, raises an important conceptual basis for understanding strategic management processes. The interconnection of perception and action is of key importance to understanding the process of building radical mental model. Mead et al. (1938) first discussed the relation of perception and action. According to them, perception, in itself, contains all elements of action. Any perceived objects are calling us to action. This "call to action" belongs to the content of our perceptual experience.

The relationship between perceptions and actions, in respect to the context of implementation of radical changes, is best explained through the prism of the perceptual cycle, developed by Neisser (1976, 20–21). As we have discussed, the perception is a constructive process, dependent on stimuli from the environment but also from our expectations versus the environment (so-called anticipatory schemes). Often, the decision maker must use the sensory system to explore the environment actively in order to gather information. The sensing system is sequentially focused on events, which are then categorized and compared with the schema from a set of anticipatory schemes. Perceptual research is completed when the selected sensory event is perceived. Then this event becomes a trigger to change the existing anticipatory schemas to new. In other words, the result of sensory research modifies the original scheme. The modified scheme determines further exploration of information and forms a perceptual sequence. The connection of form and content is obvious in the case of mental scheme. Information that meets the format in one moment of the cycle process become part of the format for the second sequence, and thus determines how the next information will be accepted. As Neisser puts it: "The schema is not only a plan but also the executor of the plan. It is a pattern of action as well as a pattern for action" (56).

In the act of realization of their ideas, people create their reality. In other words, the mental models through the activity become more defined, refined, detailed and formalized—more concrete. What the perceptual cycle highlights is that the process can be opposite—the action can trigger construction of mental models. This issue will be very important in the discussion on rhetoric of radical change. How action can consequently form mental models of the situation is described by the pragmatic instruction of William James (2007b, 321): "We need only in cold blood act as if the thing in question were real, and keep acting as if it were real, and it will infallibly end up growing in such connection with our life that it will become real." In other words, it is sufficient to allege the truth, and it will become true through its consequences.

A decision is a call for action. From my point of view, action is not only the result of cause–reaction relation but is also based on expectations that the decision maker have defined from past experience and from his perception on possible response of others to the action. At the cognitive level, the decision maker defines his situation and consequently he becomes aware of alternative actions. Since the action is goal-oriented, in other words, since it is concerned with reaching a certain subjectively perceived target, the decision maker, within the range of options available to him, will choose an action that is likely to result in what he considers to be a satisfactory result. In the same manner, the radical change follows the radical decision. Radical decision that drives radical change is defined as a new paradigm of action. Novel perspective and the initiative to achieve it start as a thinking process. It is a complex cognitive activity, consisting of asking and answering questions. The mind is active; it explores new cognitive schemata, connects it with what we already know and constructs meanings. The ability of the human mind to deal with information and direct action is what we know as competence. Competencies develop through reflection on experience.

Developing competencies through reflection

Even after the action was taken, the job with the mental models is not over. After we had done something, we can reflect on what we did and learned from it. In order to explore these issues we will tackle two themes of pivotal importance for the phenomena of bringing radical change in complex organizations—reflecting on experience which leads to change of the consecutive mental models and build problem solving competencies.

Competence is based on ability to acquire mental schemes and to recognize the interconnectedness between them. The appreciation of a complex web of cause–effect relations is primarily achieved by reflecting on our experiences and looking at what consequences one mental schemata have on the other in a particular situation and over time. As Schön (1991, 40) notes, driving from the process of mental model design, the importance of reflection on past actions and events is the key function of learning. The leader's reflection process is based on the apprehensive observation of the emotions, experiences, actions, and responses. By adding these inputs to the existing knowledge base, new knowledge and meaning are created.

The idea of the importance of reflection on the things we did is not a novel research subject. In Book II of the *Nicomachean Ethics* Aristotle asserts that the virtue can be gained only through practice: no set of rational arguments can make a person virtuous. Also, John Locke in his *Essay Concerning Human Understanding* published in 1690 (Book II) asserted that every idea is derived from experience either by sensation, by direct sensory information or by reflection.

Reflection is turning attention to our experience. The experience comes as a flow, but the only way to appreciate it is by stepping outside the stream of experience and directing our attention to it. As Weick (1995, 25) asserts: "Note that *experience* is singular, not plural. To talk about experiences implies distinct, separate episodes and pure duration do not have this quality." Actions are known only when they have been completed, which means we are always a little behind, or our actions are always a bit ahead of us. The underlying assumption of reflection as a process of learning is that mental routines (strategies acquired by experience) manage the process of gathering and interpreting evidence on which the reconstruction of the past is based (Guenther 2002; Schacter 1996). According to the constructivist theory, people use reconstructive strategies every time that they reflect on the past. We are aware of what we have done, but never while doing it. In other words, we are aware of the sensory processes, but not motor processes. Activities are known only when they end, which means we are always just a little bit behind our actions (Mead 1956; Gioia and Chittipeddi 1991). Furthermore, what happens now determines the meaning of what has already happened. The meaning is changed as the current projects and goals change.

An important notion for radical decision making is difference between "reflection-in-action" and "reflection-on-action," as contributed by Donald Schön (1991). The former is sometimes described as "thinking on our feet." It involves looking to our experiences, linking with our feelings, and getting in touch with our theories in use in order to build new understanding of the situation that is unfolding. This kind of the learning process is vividly described by Boulding (1978, 42): "Nothing fails like success, because we do not learn anything from it. We only learn from failure, but we do not always learn the right things from failure. If there is a failure of expectations, that is, if the messages that we receive are not the same as those we expected, we can make three possible inferences." Through the reflection on experience, during or after the action, the leader can improve his mental model of the decision making situation as well as become more competent to deal with another problem solving situation.

Competence is a combination of the collected factual knowledge (declarative knowledge) to be used in the right way (procedural knowledge or skills). Competencies at the expert level require superior declarative as well as procedural knowledge. The skill implies the ability to systematize information into sets or chunks, as Simon (1987) calls them, as well as to form meaningful patterns within these groups (Gobet and Simon 1996, 2000). All this provides the ability to create, store and use the cognitive schemas, which are essential building blocks of competence. The essential skill for the development of decision making competencies is the process of mental models construction. Mental modeling is used to create a virtual feedback of available scenarios that allow us to comprehend the situation more completely.

Through the prism of cognitive psychology, leading decision makers are characterized by the ability to harmonize the cognitive demands of the situation and find appropriate modes of behavior which arise from the existing schemes and experience of their use. On the other hand, beginners in decision making do not possess such patterns or fail to catch signals that indicate to some of them. Competency is defined by the number of cognitive schema of a discipline that is available to the decision maker. Mental schemas are primarily acquired through practicing. As Malcolm Gladwell (2008, 35–69) pointed out in the *Outliers*, most people that are considered to be very competent have been working at it for at least 10,000 hours. Tesla devoted thousands of hours of his childhood to studying, at great cost to any other social or leisure activities. He almost died doing it and suffered recurrent illnesses brought on by total exhaustion. Throughout his entire life Tesla claimed never to sleep more than two hours (O'Neill 1996, 293).

The competence does not refer only to the rules of discipline within which decisions are made, but also to when and how to use these rules. In other words, we are talking about the progress in the competence of the decision making in a particular discipline, but also about the "meta" decision making competence. Meta decision making competence is pure cognitive activity, independent of the discipline in which it is presented. This cognitive activity is homogeneous in the domain of the problem structuring as well as in the domain of the problem solving.

According to Baracskai, Velencei and Dörfler (2005, 20–21) we can distinguish different levels of decision making proficiency depending on the number of acquired mental schemes. The four competence levels that they have identified are novice, mediocrity, expert and master level. The novice can propose numerous schemes to solve the problem, but neither one of them is good enough. The mediocre problem solver has a large number of solutions but in the specific context he does not know how to choose one of them. An expert can choose between several solutions that would be suitable for solving a problem. And finally, the master problem solver has only one solution, precisely the one that solves the problem. The levels of knowledge are systematized in Figure 3.1. In the later work on knowledge levels by the same authors (Dörfler, Baracskai and Velencei, 2009), they have distinguished a fifth level—the grandmaster. Although the grandmaster has the same number of schemata as the master, he also has a cognitive schema that is a meta-level of all the schemes in the discipline—this is what we, usually, call wisdom. Knowledge that is used also varies within a continuum of competence development. Novice believes in everyday, commonsense reasoning. The mediocre decision maker often resorts to "objective" approach despite the fact that they are unsuitable for the problem at hand. Experts use the rules of logic in order to address the problem adequately. In contrast to the expert, at the highest level of competence, the master level has the ability to draw an overall picture of decision problems, although the process that allows him to do so cannot be expressed by words. This is because the master decision maker in his elaboration of the solution uses the language of metaphors, unlike the expert decision maker who uses technical arguments. As Prietula and Simon (1989, 121–124) note, if metaphors do not oppose our mental schemes, the master's message is acknowledged at the different levels of our consciousness which allows us to intuitively accept it as correct. As we will explore in details in the last chapter, this is the reason why the rhetoric of radical leadership is based on metaphors.

	Journeyman	Mediocre decision maker	Expert	Master
Number of schemes	10	100	1000	10000
Number of solutions	None	counless	many	one
Desides on...	the next step	cook-book	combination	image
Sees...	something else	details	rules	essence
Inference	common sense	arithmetics	logic	intuition
Language	does not speak	phrases	profession	metaphor

FIGURE 3.1 *Levels of knowledge—from journeyman to master*

4
Driving Radical Change

Abstract: *Hruška explores dynamics of radical change by focusing on two issues: mobilization for radical actions and leader's character. First, Hruška explores the driving forces behind radical decisions: deep conviction in the soundness of the radical way, commitment to the pursuit of the new governing metaphor, extreme emotional disturbance and the willingness to take risks. Special attention in understanding radical change is put on the radical leader's identity. Hruška argues that the only appropriate way of looking at the object of change is a perspective of loyalty without particular interests which, in the continuum of affection and rationality, he calls irrational optimism.*

Keywords: emotional disturbance; governing metaphor; irrational optimism; leader's identity; mobilization for radical actions; risk taking

Hruška, Domagoj. *Radical Decision Making: Leading Strategic Change in Complex Organizations.*
New York: Palgrave Macmillan, 2015.
DOI: 10.1057/9781137492319.0008.

Think different

The advertising slogan for Apple Inc—"Think different"—is the best way to describe Steve Jobs, the most influential radical decision maker in the past 20 years. Insight into his way of thinking provides useful material for understanding the mindset of radical change.

Co-founder and long-term chief executive officer of Apple Inc., Steve Jobs radically changed several industries. He introduced the Mac computers, pioneered graphical user interface, changed the way people listened to music with iTunes and the iPod, released the first-ever film created entirely with computer animation, made a radical impact on mobile phone industry by moving away from technical features and focusing on design and finally started the tablet computer industry which generates billion-dollar revenue figures for Apple on a quarterly basis.

Apple's market success comes from the fact that they adopted a new way of looking at product design—design thinking. The central premise of design thinking is not focused on aesthetic or utility, but on human cognitive apparatus and human experience. A good illustration of this is how at the age of one my son managed to make several phone calls from his mom's iPhone. The other example is how after two weeks of using the iPhone, one of my friends said: "I cannot think of going back to usual phones, nothing makes sense to me." It is very easy to find your way around Apple's products; it is like that because the design corresponds with the human cognitive apparatus. Design thinking is the radical shift in the business models of all industries in which Apple competes. The philosophy behind design thinking includes both—human thinking and behavior from one side, and technology possibilities from the other side. While the *status quo* business model focused on what the market wants and what the technology can provide, Apple decided to go in a different way. This is how Jobs described the radical change market perspective in an Inc. magazine interview in April 1989:

> I think really great products come from melding two points of view—the technology point of view and the customer point of view. You need both. You can't just ask customers what they want and then try to give that to them. By the time you get it built, they'll want something new... Yeah, and customers can't anticipate what the technology can do. They won't ask for things that they think are impossible... It sounds logical to ask customers what they want and then give it to them. But they rarely wind up getting what they really want that way.

Apple's radical business model proved to be successful. One example is the portable MP3 player industry. Although the iPod is the most well-known product in the industry, it was not the first one on the market. The first was the MPMan F10, manufactured by Korea's Saehan Information Systems, launched in March 1998. The iPod was released in November of 2001. The second example is the success in the tablet computer industry. While other companies had produced tablets as far back as the 1980s, Apple's iPad was the first tablet to accomplish significant success. Other companies could not easily copy the new business paradigm. Lack of invention and identity in competitor's business models became more visible in the light of Apple's radical approach. In a 1996 television documentary "Triumph of the Nerds" Jobs gave a diagnosis of Microsoft's critical problem: "The only problem with Microsoft is they just have no taste. They have no taste. And I don't mean that in a small way, I mean that in a big way, in the sense that they don't think of original ideas, and they don't bring much culture into their products." Apple moved from the governing metaphor of technological features to the new loadstar—design thinking—which Jobs in the aforementioned interview calls "taste."

Inaccurate nature of the radical mental models

The leader has his view of the decision making situation, his role in it as well as the roles of other organizational agents. This insight is what we call the mental model of the decision making situation. If the leader constructs a mental model whose meaning is different than the existing enacted understanding of the organization, the mental model is what we call the radically altered mental representations or the radical mental model.

As we have shown in the previous chapter, mental models have a number of limitations. For example, such models are not stable over time. The mental model that solves today's problem tomorrow may not be adequate. In addition, the stingy nature of mental models makes them useful in terms of heuristics, but not in terms of detailed action plan. This is especially true in the case of radical mental model that represent changes in the meaning of the organization, hence making people's behavior even more erratic. Moreover, the defining feature of the radical mental models is that they are not detailed and precise. The radical mental model is adaptable. It is an outlook, not a program; a set of positions and insights, not regulations or a method. This fact stems from the reference to the interpersonal and interactive nature of organizational life that is fundamental for the sensemaking process.

Members of the organization in their search for meaning should not insist on accuracy, but should find acceptable solutions. The criterion of accuracy makes more sense when we perceive an object than in the case of interpersonal perception. The usefulness of accurate objective perception is in the idea that the targets of perceptual activities have identity that does not change over time. Since the interpersonal perception is fundamental for organizational activities, one cannot take the notion of objective perception as granted. Radical decision making is quite different context than Tesla's engineering endeavors.

Realization of the radical mental model carries another issue—the problem of inaccuracy of perception that suggests we should act in spite of the inability to completely comprehend the situation. This stems from the nature of the process of search for meaning. In the search for meaning, it is not necessary to have a precise representation of the situation. Searching for meaning is about ability, pragmatism, coherence, creation and instrumentality. For these purposes, the accuracy can be an obstacle. Ericson (2001, 119–123) explains that there are three main reasons why the accuracy of perception is of secondary importance in the process of searching for meaning. The first reason is that people need to find a way to separate the signals concerning their projects from a wide range of information that engages them. From the position of search for meaning it is, therefore, more useful to observe the filters that people use in separating signals (Gigerenzer 2007) than the errors and irrationalities that are immanent to decision making (Kahneman and Tversky 1979). Another reason is that the search for meaning occurs when an extracted element of flow of experience is elaborated. Since any character has multiple meanings and importance, it is essential to find some kind of interpretation which will lead to the mobilization than to postpone the action until the "correct" interpretation appears. Weick (1995, 55–61) points out that it is illusory to insist on precision if we consider that the process of formation of meaning can use any of a number of possible characters that different decision-makers can interpreted in many different ways. The third reason why the accuracy in the search for meaning is elusive is that almost all organizational activities are time-sensitive. Speed, usually, takes a toll in precision so that rapid response shapes events before they are crystallized into specific meanings.

The more detailed the mental model is, the more precisely it can be applied. But when it comes to radical mental models, an increased level of detail can also reduce the value of the model. Insisting of accuracy of the model would reduce organizations flexibility and adaptability in the process of radical change.

There is one more reason why the accuracy is not of importance in the quest for meaning, and therefore also in the radical decision making process. That is the fact that insisting on accuracy tends to immobilize activity. "Perfectionists" in principle are not very effective. People who want to be active have a desire to simplify the world and not to elaborate it. As Brunsson (1982, 30–33) puts it—imprecise meaning is perhaps insufficient for rational decision making, but it is sufficient for the "rationality of actions."

It also needs to be pointed out that it is not only that the radical mental model is imprecise but that the correctness of the implementation of radical mental representations itself is instrumentally defined. The concept of accuracy is specific to a particular project and very pragmatic. The reason for this is that the focus on assessment of accuracy lies in the way of action that is not acceptable.

Roles of the leader in radical decision making

The presumption of good management is the overlapping of the two mental models—personal and organizational. The fact is that the most significant effect for the formation of organizational enactment has the company's top management. Still there is no guarantee that the top management has a good understanding of the organizational enactment. If the leader does not understand the enacted meaning of the organization, it may happen that he considers a particular decision radical while it really is not. The reverse situation is also possible—when the leader thinks how the decision is adaptive, and it turns out that the rest of the organization considers it to be radical. Although such situations are certainly possible, they are not frequent. They may occur in the case that the leader is a newcomer to the organization and that he makes incorrect understanding of the organization's sense before starting with intensive change. In any case, the implementation of radical decisions in such cases would be very difficult, with a lot of conflicts, resistance and a high possibility of the negative outcome.

The leader has to convince other members of the organization in the validity of the new paradigm based on novel enacted sense. If he is successful, the radical decision leads to radical change. In other case, if the leader does not have the strength to impose the radically new organizational sensemaking process, the decision will result in adaptive change, and organizational enactment will not be fundamentally altered.

The leader's main responsibility in the process is to harmonize interpretations of the radical mental model within the organization's power structure. The ability to create coalitions that support the radical decision demands understanding of the structure and institutionalization of power. The leader must invest time and energy in detecting dependencies as well as in understanding how coalitions correspond with the resources and desires that define them.

In accordance with the paradigm of social constructivism, the leader has an important influence in forming the organization's environment. The role of the leader from that point of view is to keep the pace with the environment. Tesla (2007b, 480) felt the problems of "being ahead of his time" when he said: "The practical success of an idea, irrespective of its inherent merit, is dependent on the attitude of the contemporaries. If timely it is quickly adopted; if not, it is apt to fare like a sprout lured out of the ground by warm sunshine, only to be injured and retarded in its growth by the succeeding frost."

If we take a stand that people set up their environments then, the loss of alignment between the organization and the environment gets a novel meaning. Loss of alignment might mean that the organization has developed skills, resources and constraints that have not yet been constructed in the environment. The environment requires the capabilities that the organization does not possess any longer. However, the origin of this difference lies within the organization, not outside it. The organization is changing faster than the demands it is facing. This leads us to the conclusion, voiced by Weick (2001a, 179–180) that the "problem" is not a turbulent environment, but a turbulent organization.

Radical decision making is not a process that can be comprehended from the deterministic standpoint. One of the fundamental features of the genesis of radical mental representations is that it is vague in all of its implementation elements but that at the same time the decision maker is confident in its correctness. When people are being introduced to a new idea or a new business practices, it is not possible to depict every detail of it and convince them in all its benefits. The important thing is to make them realize how we are "on their side" and that we have a story worth to be heard. If the new metaphor proposed by the leader is seen as a way to insecurity, to the events that cannot be controlled, there will be resistance. On the other hand, if a metaphor brings higher level of control over events, in other words, if it makes sense, radical change is perceived as a challenge and the resistance for its implementation is reduced.

Further on, leaders set governing metaphors for future organizational development. Smircich and Morgan (1982, 262–263) assert that setting of the governing metaphor (reference point from which process of sensemaking begins) is an important source of power in the organization. Redefinition of the reference point, for example, that the attention of members of the university is put on quality of teaching instead of quality of research and publishing, would lead to significant change in organizational dynamics. Concepts extracted from the flow of experience and used as metaphors are important because of their capacity to invoke the action. Because of this feature, search for meaning is a process that in the event of a miscalculation does not carry major consequences. In the case of any referent point, the most important element of the search for meaning is realized—stimulation of cognitive structures that leads to action. This fact changes the usual way of looking at strategy. Plans animate and orient the activities of members of the organization. Once people start to act, the action in a particular context generates tangible results which in turn helps them to find out what is happening, what remains to be explained and what to do next (Weick 1995, 54–55). This view sets the action in the center of management research. Success depends on what we did, not what we planned to do.

In the past several decades researchers have re-started thinking about traditional leadership structures that aim to understand how individuals are introducing changes in the organizational and social environment by emphasizing the role of constructing meaning in the process of leadership (Smircich and Morgan 1982; Smircich and Stubbard 1985; Pfeffer 1981;, Brehmer 1990). From that perspective, the role of the entrepreneur who starts a new enterprise is similar to the role of radical decision makers in a complex organization. The main task in both cases consists of sensemaking and sensegiving. In both situations, one must develop and convey a new mental model of business. This process starts from an existing set of mental schemes which interpret the situation, continues to develop novel perspective and to labor toward its implementation.

The search for meaning is based on finding a metaphor that leads us to the construction of safe haven for sense in the squall of otherwise meaningless elements of the environment. By finding a sense, we can "transfer" it to others. The role of leadership in the process is to persuade members to adopt a new meaning as something that they can relate to. Tao Te Ching (2012, 12) had put it well in his famous quote on leadership:

> The best leaders are those their people hardly know exist. The next best is a leader who is loved and praised. Next comes the one who is feared. The worst one is the leader that is despised... The best leader's value their words, and use them sparingly. When they have accomplished their task, the people say, "Amazing! We did it, all by ourselves!"

Of course, the wisdom of the invisible leader is not quite as simple as it might seem at first. In any case, the chances for successful implementation of the radical decision significantly increase if the leader is able to change the interpretation of the organizational agents in a way that they comprehend his mental model as their own.

As we have already noted, sensemaking and sensegiving are crucial processes for the success of top management in the process of strategic change because these cognitive competencies ultimately result with behavioral competencies. By setting novel sense of the organization, the leader is actually setting stimuli into organizational framework and drives development of cognitive maps that allows people to understand, explain, mark, assess and predict the nature of these stimuli. For example, decision makers in companies use the strategy as a framework that includes a series of actions aimed to find the meaning and direction of the organization. Louis (1980, 241) observes that setting the stimulus within the framework is best seen in the case when expectations are not met. Whenever the expectation is not confirmed, a kind of continuous action is interrupted. It also suggests that the search for meaning is under the influence of expectations. As Weick (1995, 4) puts it, to understand the search for meaning basically means to understand how people face surprises. Unexpected interruptions in the flow of experience depend on the existing organizational settings and routines, which again can be influenced by the leader.

In the process of implementation of radical changes, a leader is often faced with situations that seem unalterable. It seems that the only chance to achieve some headway is to change the hierarchy of values in the organization, in other words the organizational culture or what is sometimes referred to as the people's "mentality." This way of thinking is fundamentally flawed. As Senge et al. (2003, 271) claim, new organizational mentality cannot be straightforwardly generated; the leader can suggest new hierarchy of values that lead to new ways of doing things. Over time, the activity will open space for a new way of behavior. If the members of the organization perceive improvement in the performance of their tasks, they will readily accept the new paradigm which will ultimately result in a different view on things. In other words, the leader of radical change cannot alter the mentality, but he can prepare the grounds for its development, foster it and let it grow in an unmistakable manner of the seed. The issue is addressed in more detail in the forthcoming discussions on action based rhetoric and the process of rhetoric of radical change.

Driving forces of radical action

When we know that the leader's radical mental model is basically are vague proposition of the future state of the organization based on the novel understanding that the leader wants to enact, we can explore what preconditions need to be met in order to successfully implement wanted radical change.

Radical change is about breaking off the habitual institutional authority and persuading group to embrace novel, revolutionary ideas. Radical leaders are thus motivated to break the interpretive scheme by which people position, perceive and label occurrences in their lives consistent with the *status quo*.

Given that the radical decision fundamentally changes the default way of dealing with problems, their basic characteristics are that they cause a high level of resistance, bear great responsibility and emotional stress. Obviously it is not easy to deal with these demands, but ones we manage it, we are on the course of achieving strategic leadership. In the interview for the *Rolling Stone* magazine published June 16, 1994, Steve Jobs referred to the realization of radical change in these words:

> I have a great respect for incremental improvement, and I've done that sort of thing in my life, but I've always been attracted to the more revolutionary changes. I don't know why. Because they're harder. They're much more stressful emotionally. And you, usually, go through a period where everybody tells you that you've completely failed.

Radical leaders observe distortions and contradictions in the environment as opportunities and challenges. They feel good in situations of unstable, unclear and cognitively complex circumstances. Indeed, the radical leaders even tend to create unstable context. As Mintzberg (1973, 48) asserts, it is just such ambiguity what allows the leader to interpret the loosely structured environment and affect its elements. The successful radical decision maker is the one who can shape the future of the organization and maintain significant change processes through which his radical mental model will be accomplished.

Four attributes are crucial for successful radical decision making: deep conviction in the soundness of the radical way, commitment to the pursuit of new governing metaphor, extreme emotional disturbance, and a willingness to take the risk.

In order to go through with a radical change, the leader needs to be confident in the rightness of the wider picture in which the radical change is framed. The perspective is considered to be "larger than life"—more important than fulfillment of personal goals. Deciding to go through with a radical decision is principally of selfless character. As the other people, by definition, do not understand, and therefore do not approve changes that radical decision bear, the change is not made for the sake of popularity but because of a deep conviction that it is needed. Abraham Lincoln (Basler 1989, 607) illustrates this well in one particularly sublime passage of his address to Congress in which he describes the Civil War as "a struggle for maintaining in the world, that form, and substance of government, whose leading object is to elevate the conditions of men—to lift artificial weights from all shoulders—to afford all, an unfettered start, and a fair chance, in the race of life."

There is, however, one case in which introduction of radical change can have a different origin. That is the case when the leader wants to change enacted meaning of the organization in order to integrate momentarily scattered interpretations. This kind of "team building" instrumentalization of radical change is a powerful tool in the leader's toolkit although also potentially a very dangerous one.

Most of the approaches to decision making do not involve emotions (Damásio 2005). Still, emotions play a key role in the process. They are the foundation of all mental processes and triggers of action. One of the key ways to understand the organizational sensemaking process is to comprehend how people usually act according to their emotions and shape the context in which they retroactively seek for meaning which allows them to understand why they made the decision in a first place. The importance of emotions in the formation of mental models also reflect in the fact that the implementation of decisions are grounded in emotions as well since people seldom *know*, but always feel. Radical decisions bear high emotional agitation because of their "do or die" character. Although not always pleasant, this emotional boost proves to be very helpful at the early stage of implementation of radical change. Kahneman (1973, 28), for instance, noted that arousal influences the total attention capacity in any given situation. In general, emotional exaltation increases one's commitment to follow true with the solving of the problem.

Emotions are helpful in the process of radical decision making, but their defining attribute is that they cannot be controlled. Therefore, the leader has to include one thing that he can influence—his will. The leader's commitment to the implementation of radical change is a necessary part of the process.

The radical mental model needs to be continuously confirmed through the activity of the people in the organization. As we have said, the initial radical mental model is incomplete, so it does not allow the leader to depict future developments in detail. It is the leader's action that opens strategic continuum and brings about new material for sensemaking. So the only way for a leader to implement radical change is to make sure that expected consequences of his moves successively confirm initial radical mental model. The belief in the correctness of radical decision's broad vision and the leader's continuous commitment to its confirmation through the activity are the very reasons why it is possible to implement radical change. The incompleteness of the radical mental model also influences the implementation of radical change in a way that it is not possible to know with certainty whether a specific concrete decision is actually a good way to go or not. But despite that, the radical change still can be implemented, because the expected consequences of the decisions confirm the leader's radical mental model.

In order to take a radical decision the leader needs to congregate a sufficient level of courage. The threshold for making radical decisions varies from individual to individual and depends on the perception of risks attached to the decision. In order to reduce the perceived risk in the process of radical change leaders can utilize several mechanisms. Through these mechanisms, the leader will be able to create a context that would facilitate the development of profound organizational changes. First, the perception of risk can be diminished by the exploration of the consequences of the radical decision through the visualization of all possible scenarios. The leader will be able to comprehend the worst and the best possibilities, especially the worst, and will be able to make preparations in the case of different scenarios. The second way to enable a leader to make radical decisions is to ensure his existential security. Radical decisions are risky business. If the decision maker needs to worry about his existential needs, it is likely that he will make moves that are less risky. The third mechanism for diminishing risk attached to the radical decision is ensuring the support of key organizational stakeholders. Radical decisions cannot be made unless they are made by the locus of control of the organization. That is why organizations whose control is based on fragile alliances very seldom can be the object of radical change. That also goes for most of the governmental organizations that are by definition amalgams of opposing interests.

Leader's identity for radical change

Driving forces that we have just elaborated stem from the attributes of a radical decision. They point to the things the leader has to be prepared for if he is about to take radical action. Leaning on influences of radical change for the people who go through it, this part of the description of the radical ways poses the question of leader's identity. More concrete, this part of the book deals with explication of a number of specific characteristics that a leader must combine in order to pursue a radical kind of organizational change.

Identity, or the accepted definition of being who or what someone is, is a concept that nearly everyone has struggled with at some point. Identity is about roots of all our thinking and action. It is a question of "what we believe in," "what we do," and "what we are." Identity gives us a vision, but also the strength to achieve the vision.

At a specific moment in time everybody has an identity, an underlying philosophy of his thoughts and actions. People always believe in something. So the question we ask here is—what should a leader who wants to implement radical change believe in? It is a hard question. In order to answer it we will explore four other issues: why the leaders actually have to believe, what are the reasons and pitfalls of identity shifts, why the leaders should not believe in themselves and finally what are the most important attributes of a leader's identity for implementation of radical organizational change.

Identity is a question of devotion to the idea, person, thing or place. This devotion is the source of creative energy. Strong sense of identity opens creative energy that enables more effective and efficient results. The importance of identity is highlighted by the fact that the strong sense of identity is one of the characteristics of long-lived organizations (de Geus 1997, 9). In the instrumental sense, there is no difference between an individual's identity and the identity of the organization. In both cases, identity provides an answer to the same question. What defines our thinking and acting? In other words what is our enacted meaning—the expression of identity?

As we said before, everybody believes in something but if our devotion to the object of our belief is not strong enough, we will not be able to keep strategic continuity and our current efforts will in time prove to be useless. Therefore, in radical decision making, the leader needs to focus his beliefs as much as possible. What we choose as the core of our identity is what defines us in the most profound way. Whatever that is, it works as a constraint, as a limitation. But in a seemingly paradoxical way, the more constraints we have, the more creative we can be. This notion is vividly described by Stravinsky (1970, 65) in his work *Poetics of Music*:

> My freedom thus consists in my moving about within the narrow frame that I have assigned myself for each one of my undertakings. I shall go even further: my freedom will be so much the greater and more meaningful the more narrowly I limit my field of action and the more I surround myself with obstacles. Whatever diminishes constraint diminishes strength. The more constraints one imposes, the more one frees one's self of the chains that shackle the spirit.

The heart has to be committed in order for our hands to be free.

A strong identity means that in the situation of confrontation and crisis it will not change, but will remain to be the fundament of our thinking and action. If we are determined to keep the identity in every occasion, we will soon be challenged. One of the most important topics in organizational psychology is how the collective influences formulation of one's identity. According to Erez and Earley (1993, 28), our understanding of ourselves is a creation that primarily stems from three needs. First is a need for self-improvement, based on the pursuit and maintenance of positive cognitive and affective understanding of oneself. Second is the personal effectiveness which is a desire to be seen as a competent and effective person. Third need is the need for self-sustainability—the need to feel and experience the coherence and continuity. Although this perspective offers an adequate explanation for most of the organizational life, it is not suitable for our radical needs. For the radical leader, rootedness has to lie in something other than the social.

There are two ways to change the identity. First one is that the leader changes his identity willingly because he thinks that new "software" will be more effective or more interesting. In radical change processes this kind of behavior is often fatal. A leader cannot be modern, in the sense that he changes his attitudes all the time according to the present whims of the audience. This kind of deliberate change of identity happens very often and is a matter of desire to serve the idolatry of the collective. As Weil (2002, 125) writes: "A Pharisee is someone who is virtuous out of obedience to the Great Beast." The Great Beast, the collective, is always hungry; we can spend hundreds of lives feeding it, and it would still ask for more.

Second is that the leader changes his identity as a result of outside influences, primarily through interaction. In respect to the first way of identity shift, a leader is not willingly changing his identity but is manipulated into it by "the collective." In this way, identities are constructed through the process of interaction. It seems that this way of identity construction is a default process; we need to use energy to keep working and thinking under command of a stable identity. In this default situation, each decision maker is parliament in him as Mead (1934, 255–256) says. We are different people when we talk with family members, and different when we talk with our boss. The character of those in whose eyes we see ourselves carries a big impact on how we feel and consequently what we think about ourselves. We always imagine, and in imagining we absorb the estimates of others. This process consequently forms our identity but only until new experience. The process can be depicted by the well-known sales lesson—when is the seller in the best mood to make a good deal? Right after he closed one.

It seems that the more transcendental and complex the origin of a leader's identity is, the better it is. What we believe in cannot be some outward fad. It must be a governing metaphor that builds all of our sensemaking processes. Focusing on practical issues for identity building is not a good approach. We cannot hold the weight of ambiguity and uncertainty that radical change brings. The building material is just not flexible enough. For radical decision maker, the identity must be based on a matter of transcendent quality. This is probably one of the reasons why all of the people who earned huge sums of money never say that they did it for the money. The more transcendental our sense of loyalty is, the more practical is our policy.

Second, what the radical leader believes in should not be some compromise but the most important issues at the peak of their effectiveness. In his "Doctrine of the Mean," Aristotle (1893) is making the point that the important thing, as far as moral virtue is concerned, is to act appropriately to the situation, without overreacting (excess) or underreacting (deficiency) to a particular set of circumstance. For instance, in the sphere of feelings between fear and confidence, one can overreact, vice of rashness, or underreact, vice of cowardice, while the right way to address the situation is through the virtue of courage. Although Aristotle's Doctrine might be, as it often has been, interpreted as a moral recommendation that proper moral behavior consists in always acting moderately or without excessive feeling, this is not what he says. He clearly states that his theory how the virtue lies between extremes is not intended as a procedure for making decisions, but just as an illustration for understanding which qualities of character are actually virtues. It seems to me that he actually does not speak about mean between two extremes, but both extremes in collision out of which the specific kind of balance is formed. Courage is also such a paradox—in order to stay alive we have to embrace the possibility of death. Courage is what gives strength to the soul to pass through the breaking point, without breaking. Peaceful collision of opposing passions forms much more suitable framework for radical reforms than compromise between two vices. Because of our radical goals of revolution, what we need is not the cold acceptance, in a way of a compromise, but finding a way by which we can honestly hate it and honestly love it.

Before I give a proposition of the suitable cornerstones of radical decision maker's identity, I want to emphasize one more thing. Whatever we pick to believe in is better than to believe only in ourselves. Do not believe in yourself? Coming from a management scholar, this certainly sounds like a heretical doctrine. Most of the business administration literature, as well as the overall understanding of business, is based on the notion of self-confidence. But if we take a closer look at the matter of self-confidence we will see that its role is often misinterpreted. As Chesterton (1908, chap. 2, 1) vividly puts it:

> If you consulted your business experience instead of your ugly individualistic philosophy, you would know that believing in himself is one of the commonest signs of a rotter. Actors who can't act believe in themselves; and debtors who won't pay. It would be much truer to say that a man will certainly fail because he believes in himself.

In radical decision making, as well as in most other organizational activities, we have a very large number of possibilities that something will not go as we planned. In that situation, complete self-confidence is a weakness. A leader's identity should not be based on his strengths. Faith in oneself implies faith in his intellect and his will. Both of them can prove to be completely wrong roadmaps.

If we examine people who base their identity on faith in their intellect, we can see several things. First, expansive and detailed logic prevents them from making creative efforts and changing their attitude. Second, these kinds of people do not possess the slightest irresolution and thus they do not possess the necessary complexity. Third, given that the world is complex, their scope of the use of reason is very limited.

The problem of faith in reason can be illustrated by the characteristics of its extreme that is complete determinism. Materialism of this sort is based on the crazy feeling of simplicity that flow is represented by a chain of causality. Its biggest problem is that this detailed and logical mental construction gradually destroys human nature. Polanyi (1964, 4–5) reveals this when he asserts how "we abandon the cruder anthropocentrisms of our senses—but only in favor of a more ambitious anthropocentrism of our reason." There is no hope, initiative, courage, goodness and everything else that defines a human being. The other extreme of speculative logic would be a man who does not believe in anything but himself. This concept, same as our faith in ratio, is complete in theory but flawed in practice. The man who cannot trust his own senses and a man who can trust only to his senses have the same problem—each is closed in his perspective and cannot get out. Objective intellectualism is a weakness if it is used without merits, if it does not reflect transcendentalism.

The same can be said for the will. A common view on the will is that it is an act, something that expands and breaks. But in principle, it is the opposite. Chesterton (1908, chap. 3, 7) makes this point when he says:

Every act of will is an act of self-limitation. To desire action is to desire limitation. In that sense every act is an act of self-sacrifice. When you choose anything, you reject everything else...Just as when you marry one woman you give up all the others, so when you take one course of action you give up all the other courses.

Basing our identity in our will consequently leads us to neglect all laws and constraints. We become a rebel that does not have any loyalty and therefore cannot carry the revolution. By standing up against everything, the rebel has lost the right to stand up against anything.

In the context of radical decisions, faith in the lawlessness will and materialistic faith in the law of reason ends up in the same way. The materialist will not go ahead with the decision because his logic does not allow him to see the benefits of extraordinary action. Also, the rebel will not make a decision because for him all extraordinary actions are worth doing. Complete faith in ourselves, in our will or in our ratio consequently has the same effect—impotency.

With this discussion, I also want to discard the myth of the radical decisions maker as the all-powerful leader-hero character. According to this paradigm, radical leadership would be limited to few individuals with the extraordinary abilities. As Senge et al. (2003, 7–8) describe, they have become leaders because of the special combination of skills, ambition, charisma and confidence. In accordance with the myth, to achieve a radical change it is necessary that the process is carried by one of these "Übermensch." It is not so. On the contrary, if this is the case, radical decision making would be almost disabled. It is precisely the worship of the super-leaders cult what inevitably makes institutions unwilling to accept change because the "ordinary people" do not have a chance to make significant changes. With regard to the effect of self-fulfilling prophecy, there is almost no better way to maintain the *status quo*. Thus, in the long run, the price paid for nurturing the idea that every change must be carried out by the "superman" is extremely high.

In addition to everything stated earlier, belief in oneself has one more, very serious consequence—hubris. The terrible outlook of the faith in oneself is very appealing to the mystical egoism of our time. People are rushing for the "Übermensch" and set themselves above everyone and everything. "Pride makes oneself into a proud little god," as McCloskey (2006, 103) writes. I will not mention here obvious social consequences of pride, but the one that deals with construction of radical mental models. An overbearing man looks at everything from a bird's eye perspective, and from there everything seems small and insignificant. In this respect, he does not have real understanding of the situation or the impression of its complexity. Besides such a view is not at all interesting, the egoist cannot retrieve the necessary information to create the radical mental models. The proud man never gets to change, at least not by his strengths.

Reasonable question at this stage is—if I shouldn't believe in myself, what should I believe in? In the heart of my identity, I should have ideals that depict what kind of man I want to be. It is not about having faith in me but in the man I want to be. So even when sometimes I fall short and do not make it, the ideal still stands and reminds me what I have to do tomorrow. What applies for leaders applies for the organizations—the seemingly paradoxical conclusion that a solid base in terms of stable value makes organization more flexible (Senge et al. 2003, 270). The sense of identity based on values enables companies to identify less with the current situation within and outside the company

A solid and familiar ideal is required for each revolution. What should be the foundation of a leader's faith in respect to radical decision making? Coming from the nature of radical decision making, I had identified five principles that together depict the identity for execution of radical change: fortitude, perseverance, cooperation, care for others and humbleness.

Fortitude stands for the fact that the leader cannot compromise his principles. What a man believes in depends on his philosophy, not on the situation he is in. It can be often heard that "one must compromise." It is true that in radical decision making the leader has to pick his fights carefully, but compromise cannot be made on the key concepts of the radical mental model. If the leader starts the radical change without firmness in his interpretation of the governing metaphor of novel organization, he might consider himself defeated before the start.

Perseverance is the principle that helps us finish the task when the flames of our initial enthusiasm die down. In radical decision making, we are asked for the heroism of ending the responsibilities committed to us properly. When the problems start, people have a tendency to change the vision because it is much easier than to keep trying to solve the issue. The principle of perseverance is also tested in the leader's congruence. If the leader does not live what he preaches, he will not be believed.

The third principle of leadership for radical change is cooperation. It is well known that mediocre men surround themselves by thoughtless people when they are in power. Their pride fallaciously persuades them how, that way, they will never lose control. Radical leaders have to be cognitively and emotionally ready for collaboration; they have to surround themselves with wise people that would give them advice and support. Steve Jobs nicely proves the point in his elaboration of the things that have allowed him to succeed in the 1984 *Access Magazine* interview: "Well, you know, there were probably a lot of guys out there sitting in garages who thought, 'Hmmm, let's make a computer.' Why did we succeed? I think we were very good at what we did, and we surrounded ourselves by very fine people." The radical decision maker has to foster and cultivate interdependencies because he understands that in making others great he will not lose anything, on the contrary.

The radical decision maker should have profound care for other people in the organization—attention to people's individual needs as well as respect for their unique circumstances and concerns. One might ask—what about situations when the radical change means layoffs? Yes, even then. Especially then. The leader has all organization to take care off. And his primary role is to persuade people to change their minds in a way to embrace a new governing metaphor of the business model. To feel protected by the affectionate understanding of the one in charge is always effective help in this process.

The last principle is the most important one. Radical decision makers should always stay humble. All your knowledge, eloquence and power, if you are not humble, are worth nothing. This might sound a bit dramatic but let us not forget that the arena for radical change is first and foremost in minds of the people and all people are tuned to recognize arrogance.

These principles, as well as the organizational radical decision making altogether, are for those who want to fight. The weak, the lazy, the cunning, the cowardly and the arrogant will fail.

Irrational optimist of radical leadership

When we have examined the desirable traits of a leader's identity for driving radical organizational change, we have only one more thing to do—to study leader's attitude toward the object of change.

When we look at the organization, we can look at it from two perspectives—it is worth the effort or it is not. Either we are devoted to the organization or we are not. We can say, for lack of a better word, that we are either optimists or pessimists. Also, we can be either with or without concrete reason for it. So, as showed in Figure 4.1, in examining a leader's attitude toward the object of radical change, two things are of importance—our loyalty (or lack of it) and our reasons for this. The dimensions of loyalty and rationality form the continuum in which we can observe the underlying philosophy of radical action.

The bigger the reform that we want to implement, the bigger the pledge of loyalty that has to be made. When we speak of loyalty, we are talking about love. "Loyalty" is a better word than "love" because our focus is on the desire to conduct change. We cannot radically change anything if we do not feel any loyalty toward it, but we can change it, and in principle we often do, if we feel enmity. Even if we honestly hate something with the intention to change it, it is still loved enough to be considered worth changing. Love and hate are sometimes close. Change driven by love can almost always be seen in romantic relationships. A woman stops trying to change a man only when she ceases to love him.

Pessimists do not have loyalty. There are two possible turn of events in this case. The pessimist can stop being part of the organization altogether, or he can participate in it as long as it suits him, even until, in his perspective, its inevitable end. Our major concern, however, is not in the action but in the underlying philosophy. If we are pessimists, if we think that the organization is not something we should care about, we might think that because of two reasons. We might do our math—quantify, interpret, mitigate risk and find that is not worth a shot. On the other hand, we can just say that it is not going to work because, well, we just hate the idea. I call this kind of people rational and irrational pessimists.

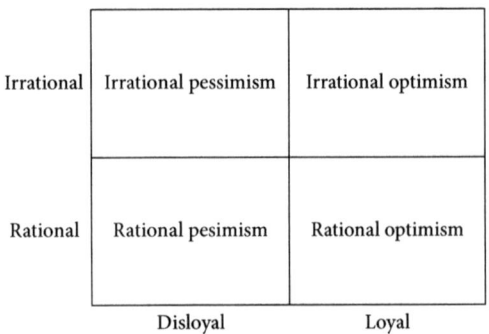

FIGURE 4.1   *A leader's attitude toward the object of radical change*

Pessimists, however, are not of interest for our debate. We are more concerned with optimists—with the people who are devoted to the organization and who can use the loyalty as a fuel for change. In respect to the reasons for loyalty, I can also identify two approaches as I did in the pessimist case. The first reason for loyalty to the organization is specific. This kind of thinking is what I call rational optimism. Potential reasons for rational optimism are many: I enjoy my work environment, I manage my business process with ease, the pay is excellent and pension plan is great, to name just a few. A rational optimist owes his allegiance to the existing state of the organization; he likes it just the way it is, and he will not want to change it radically. Such a leader will be less inclined to reform things, and more inclined to some official, petty political response that would justify the status quo. Even in situations when the radical reform would be needed, the rational optimist would always insist on changing just the little things. Progress of this kind of the decision maker comes down to the adaptive decisions and as such, the rational optimist is not able to bring his organization into the position of strategic leadership.

On the other hand, irrational optimism is when a person loves for no reason. We do not love the organization because of the perks, but because of what it represents on the more abstract level. As we have noted earlier, the more abstract our devotion is, the more drastic and far-reaching its restructuring can be. Irrational optimism is the only psychology that allows radical change. It is a kind of feeling that is perhaps best described by the notion of patriotism as Chesterton (1908, chap. 5, 2) defines it: "Men did not love Rome because she was great. She was great because they had loved her." Irrational optimism is about love for what the organization can be and not for what it is at the moment. In short, the leader, in order to implement a radical change, must praise the object of change to the extent that she is willing to change it completely. If the leader is attached to the part of the existing situation, she will not seek radical change. In order for a change to be radical, the leader's commitment must be directed to the idea behind the petty individual interests.

5
The Loadstar

Abstract: *In this chapter Hruška gives insight into the adherent steps in the development of the radically different mental representations. Concerning the origins of new concepts, the three issues are apostrophized: a novelty of concept; a degree of novelty for different people; origins of novel concepts—their embedding in mental models and the nature of the relation between concepts and conceptual structures. Hruška also elaborates the use of metaphors in the process of developing organization and management theories. Special focus is on the genesis of the governing metaphor of radical decision making that Hruška calls a "Loadstar."*

Keywords: governing metaphor; loadstar; novel concepts; radical mental model

Hruška, Domagoj. *Radical Decision Making: Leading Strategic Change in Complex Organizations.*
New York: Palgrave Macmillan, 2015.
DOI: 10.1057/9781137492319.0009.

The journey

One of the most engaging biblical narratives is the one of the journey of the three wise man from "the East." The story has important connotations for a radical decision making in respect to the leading metaphor of new, radical mental model.

As Christians believe, the son of God, Jesus from Nazareth, was born in Bethlehem, and soon after the birth the three pilgrims from the east arrived to pay tribute to the baby that would change the history of the world. The biblical story of the three magi that sought Christ offers valuable insight into the nature of high stake endeavors.

Matthew's gospel is the only one of the four Canonical gospels to mention the wise men. The magi were probably members of the Persian priest caste. They were people of hope, people of inner unrest that undertook the adventurous and risky journey in search of the true light—*lux vera*. Just as Abraham, father of the three monotheistic religions, started his journey at the call of God, so are the magi set on the way by their religious and philosophical wisdom.

The wise men were guided to look for the King of the Jews by a miraculous stellar event, the "Star of Bethlehem," which they called "His star" (Matt. 2:2). The loadstar was probably a real astronomical event, but that real event was interpreted by the *magi* and ultimately led them to their goal. The conjunction of planets Jupiter and Saturn in the zodiac sign of fish, which took place in the years 6–7 BC, would direct the Babylonian astronomers toward the land of Judas. That solution was presented by Johannes Kepler and is still the main explanation of the story. So, the magi could be astronomers who were looking for a sign, but it would not be enough of an incentive to undergo such an expedition. For a conjunction to send a message, there would have to be a story or prophecy of a kind. It seems that in the time these kinds of expectations were present. Ratzinger (2012, 109) mentions that historian Joseph Flavius connected this prophecy with the emperor Vespasian and hence managed to gain his affection.

The star could be the first sign, initial external incentive for departure. However, it would not be enough if they were not touched by inner incentive—the hope. Most likely, the magi knew of the writings of the prophet Daniel (9:24–27), who had been the high seer at the court in Persia, that includes a prophecy which gives a timeline for the birth of the Messiah. Also, the magi may have been aware of the prophecy of pagan prophet Balaam (Num. 24:17). Balaam's prophecy specifically mentions a "star coming out of Jacob"—meaning the geographic area of Judea, mountainous southern part of the historic Land of Israel (Ratzinger 2012, 104–105).

The wise men started the journey following the loadstar which took them to Judea, where they consulted with the king of Judea and the religious scriptures. After the consultations with King Herod in Jerusalem concerning the birth of Christ they were directed to Bethlehem (Matt. 2:4–8). It is interesting that once they reached Jerusalem, the star has descended but after they collected information from the scripture it came out once again (Matt. 2:9): "After they had heard the king, they went on their way, and the star they had seen when it rose went ahead of them until it stopped over the place where the child was." Last, it is interesting to note that the Gospel says that they followed God's guidance joyfully (Matt. 2:10): "When they saw the star, they were overjoyed." It is the joy of the one who believed and hoped and reached the goal.

The loadstar was a sign, a metaphor that guided actions of the three wise man. They were intrinsically motivated to find the newborn. They dared to take very dangerous trip in order to follow something they believed in. We can imagine that their trip would be laughed at by some of their peers, but still they moved ahead with it. The decision to start a journey was implemented in an incremental manner. They were following the star, looking for the signs from the scriptures, asking for direction. All the time, even when the star has descended, they believed that they would reach their goal. All radical decisions are such. A leader has to have a governing metaphor, a loadstar out of which he constructs a mental model that he enacts in reality through his actions. The role of this chapter is to discuss the nature and genesis of the governing metaphor.

The new

There are so many books about creativity and innovation. Rationalization of the emergence of new concepts is the aspiration of authors from almost all disciplines of knowledge and art—from philosophy and theology to physics and poetry. Throughout centuries great thinkers such as Plato, Locke, Hume, Bacon and Popper, to name just a few, discussed the issue of the *new*. Still, fundamental questions about the process are not answered. As Schön (1963, 3) points out theories of concept development tend to fall in one of two categories—either the process is considered intrinsically inexplicable (mysterious) because the novelty is creation *ex nihilo* or it is deemed to be illusory because things stay essentially the same and the process, therefore, does not require explanation.

Concerning the novelty of concepts, three issues are important in respect to radical decision making: not all concepts are new to all people, how new something actually is and from where we actually constitute "the new."

Obviously, the concept can be new to one person while the other is already familiar with it. An anecdote says that when Europeans arrived on Hawaii islands, they brought cattle with them. Since there are no indigenous cattle on Hawaii, the native people were simply terrified of the cows and horses. Supposedly, the bravest Hawaiian warrior has run away screaming after an encounter with a cow. It is not that the concept did not exist before; it is just that we do not have experience with it. Psychology of cognitive development is most focused on children. Nowhere is the notion of *new* so clearly present. My son is just getting to know how the concept of stairs has the unfortunate characteristic of falling down from them. It seems that in many cases knowing is not enough—just knowledge rarely change our conceptual structures. What we need is an authentic experience. Or more precisely, as we previously noted, reflection on our experience. For me, a new concept is the one which emerges for the first time for an individual, regardless of his culture.

Second, the changes are a matter of degree. Some changes are easily recognized; they are only minor variations of an old theme, and we can easily cope with them. The recognition of the underlying theme and the surprise in interpretation of transitions are probably what makes jazz music so interesting to some people. On the other hand, some concepts are fundamentally different than the ones we have experience with. The new concept is the one which is unexpected, which comes up for the first time. As such, it is always a subject of attention. It becomes a subject of resistance when we try to embed it into the working mental models.

The third thing about the new concepts that I want to point out is their origin. Answering the question will also point out to the way how we, usually, use them. Since the concepts are understood as expectations through which we structure out experience, as we have discussed in the previous chapter, it becomes clear that concepts and theories of action cannot be separated. However, in the previous discussion about the structure of mental models I did not mention one thing that I want to point out now—the concepts are not mental structures superimposed on experience. So the theories of action are not built out of concepts. The process is reversed. To discuss formulation of new theories of action, that is, the new sets of expectations for coping with the world, is to discuss the formulation of new concepts. We separate concept from existing flow of experience and post it into the novel surroundings where it defines novel meaning. When an author puts his idea on the paper, he actually separates himself from it. Same analogy is a woman that brings a child to the world. Every act of creation is an act of separation.

Metaphors and theories

The creation of "new" is a process based on the use of metaphors. Any representation of the creative principle must be metaphorical because it must be verbal. The term "metaphor" has a wide variety of partly related and partly incompatible meanings. Probably, the most well-known definition of the term would be that it is a linguistic expression where one or more words for a concept are used outside of its normal conventional meaning to express a different meaning. The definition of the term, as well as the use of metaphors, is apt to be confusing.

We can say that metaphors can be treated as a piece of language or as a process of thought. In the first sense, a metaphor is a word that brings to mind more than a single reference, and several references are seen to have something in common (Brown 1958). On the other hand, metaphor can be seen as a verbal expression that leads to metamorphosis of experience (Cassirer 1946).

In use of metaphors, the symbolic relation is the exclusive one. The symbolic relation is vague and mysterious. It allows the indefinite number of possible specifications. If we take symbolic relation as the principal relation between terms and their references, we lose the notion of single meaning. That has troublesome consequences for theories of truth. It is not, however, much of a problem in common sense of ordinary practice. We know what it means when we say that King Arthur had his knights sit at a round table or what is a key identity trait of Richard the Lionheart.

Metaphors bear witness to complex processes of deconstruction and construction of concepts and their symbolic connections. Instead of just retrieving frames or verbally exclaimed relationships between concepts, metaphorical language sets up a creative and often novel correlation of two concepts within the mental model which forces us to make semantic leaps to create an understanding of the information that comes off it (Coulson 2001, 3). The main enabler of this process is the fact that concepts are capable of entering into relations with an unlimited variety of other ideas or concepts, rather than a limited set of predefined categories.

The use of metaphors in organizations is about theory construction and theorizing. Organization and management theories are about predicting turn of events in complex settings. Concepts stem from conceptual structures which are of the cognitive nature and which we call mental models. They are set in action by linguistic or another sort of expressions that convey certain meaning. Even if this movement is of the symbolic nature it allows us to navigate through the realm of experience and devise our response to the situation in hand. The response itself is actually a theory, a theory of action in complex setting.

So in the decision making situation we are faced with the theories of action. The search for meaning, however, can be focused within several different frames: in the case of whole society we use ideologies, within the organizations we use the control mechanisms of the third order, within the various professions we use paradigms, within the process of learning from previous situations we use tradition and within the gained experience we use narratives (Tsoukas and Hatch 2001).

Interpretations of organizations are always based on some sort of theory to explain reality. The organizational reality can be understood in terms of several perspectives. Some people only see the organization in terms of one metaphor, and some are able to recognize several perspectives. As we will discuss a bit later, in order to open his mind to diverse interpretations one needs to suspend judgment, for the most part by dealing with his ego.

Many authors have emphasized the use of metaphor as a cognitive and heuristic device in organization studies (Morgan 1980; Morgan, Frost and Pondy 1983; Tsoukas 1991; Cornelissen 2006, 2004; Weick 1989). All these theories of organization are based on implicit images or metaphors that stretch out imagination in an attempt to experiment with potentially helpful solutions. The ability to integrate new metaphors helps with the conceptualization of the task and is essential for people involved in leadership and organizational change.

As already noted, the book looks at organizational theorizing as an ongoing and evolutionary process. The perspective poses that the concept of organization and explanation of organizational life relies heavily on the foundation of metaphorical description. This approach was explained in a most detailed account in Karl Weick's (1989, 516) article on theory construction by the use of what he calls "disciplined imagination." Weick argues that people in organizations are both a source of variation and the source of selection in each instance of theory construction, or, in other words, in each action they consider. In constructing theory, Weick suggested, people rely upon metaphors to provide them with incentives (mainly vocabularies and images) to make sense of the organizational phenomena. In their attempt to understand the situation in hand, people use their imagination by setting different metaphors in action in their cognitive apparatus. The metaphor is the vehicle through which imagination takes place and as a source for theoretical representations. The various metaphorical inputs are then further selected through the application of specific selection criteria and retained for further use. In an insightful manner, Weick notes that such a process of theory construction resembles the three processes of evolution: variation, selection and retention.

The "disciplined imagination" notion has an important role in our discussion. In a nutshell—with the use of metaphors, leaders can simulate theories of action and find solutions for organizational problems. Radical change, however, demands one addition to the perspective—the issue of metaphor's influence on the creation of meaning. Metaphors convey concentrated meaning that gives them a central position in the sensemaking process. In order to find the solution of the problem in hand, the leader can decide to experiment with metaphorical inputs of peripheral importance in the creation of meaning. The problem might be solved, but the meaning of the situation stays the same. On the other hand, the new metaphor can replace the very central notion of the situation's sensemaking process. If that is the case, the new metaphor is a loadstar of radical decision making.

Metaphors have one more important role in the implementation of radical change. Due to the fact that words are the poor medium for the transmission of meaning, metaphors represent the foundation of communication of radically changed perspectives to the organization members. Each situation is a part of the individual's world. If we acknowledge the constructivist perspective, we need to bear in mind that each "world" has its own language that the leader needs to "talk" to in order to influence the mental construction of the involved people.

The leader must send his message in a form that is acceptable to all or at least to most of the organization members. If this form were largely unambiguous large number of members of the organization would not be able to correspond with it. For this reason, the leader uses a form that each member of the organization can fit into his mental model—a metaphor. Metaphors allow people to focus at the desired direction but also to tolerate a sufficient level of flexibility in the interpretation, which is a prerequisite for the effective implementation of radical change.

The governing metaphor

As noted, in the process of mental model construction there are concepts that are central to the understanding and the ones which are of peripheral importance. In the heart of the mental model derived by the process of sensemaking is a single concept most intimately tied to others, crucial to the whole system of understanding and most anxiously guarded. The concept is a metaphor because it conveys the seed of meaning that can flourish in numerous ways in people's minds. It is called the "governing metaphor."

After Paul O'Neill had been appointed as the CEO of aluminum manufacturing giant Alcoa, he said that the company will not be focusing on revenues or R&D anymore but that it will have a new focus—safety. The new focus proved to be very successful, and O'Neill's emphasis didn't just increase safety but changed the company. A year after the radical shift, profits hit a record high, and when O'Neill retired 13 years later, the company's annual net income was five times higher than at the beginning of his term. Transformation of the company started with one key element, a new metaphor. As O'Neill states, in the 2014 *Business Insider* article: "I knew I had to transform Alcoa. But you can't order people to change. So I decided I was going to start by focusing on one thing. If I could start disrupting the habits around one thing, it would spread throughout the entire company."

The theoretical framework used for describing the role of a governing metaphor in radical decision making is the model first introduced by William James back in 1890 (2007b, 340–343), and then reinvented in organizational psychology within Karl Weick's (1995, 49–55) work on organizational sensemaking. The idea behind the model is how meaning is constructed on the basis of one mental schemata, one character selected from the overall flow of experience. The extracted character is a simple, familiar structure from which we build a sense of a specific problem situation. They combine all the elements of the observed situation and govern the process of sensemaking. The process is the same with the simplest problem solving situations such as deciding what to have for breakfast and with the most complex ones. For instance, this is how James (2007a, 8), in the introduction of his seminal work *The Principles of Psychology*, describes deepest of all philosophical problems:

> Is the Kosmos an expression of intelligence rational in its inward nature, or a brute external fact pure and simple? If we find ourselves, in contemplating it unable to banish the impression that it is a realm of final purposes, that it exists for the sake of something, we place intelligence in the heart of it and have a religion. If on the contrary, in surveying its irremediable flux we can think of the present only as so much mere mechanical sprouting from the past, occurring with no reference to the future, we are atheist and materialist.

Process of understanding is a question of being "unable to banish" single concept, a metaphor that carries meaning.

There are two basic orientations in organizational research concerning the form of the methodological approach to the study of metaphor (Cornelissen et al. 2008). The first one is cognitive or "de-contextual" approach to metaphor—it stresses that metaphors function as organizing principles of thought and experience. The second one tends to "contextualize" metaphors at their locally specific uses and meanings as well as to their interaction with other elements of discourse. Most researchers use the "de-contextual approach" and deal with metaphors from the perspective of an organization as a consistent sensemaking arena (Morgan 1980, 2006; Putnam and Boys 2006; Palmer and Dunford 1996). Position of these researchers is how an organization's governing metaphor directs people to a specific kind of behavior and thinking. One can better understand organizations by recognizing that action theories are based on metaphors that prompt an individual to view the organization through a particular lens. For instance, Morgan (2006) suggested that organizations are built on one of the following metaphors: machine, organism, brain, culture, political system, psychic prison, flux and transformation, and instruments of domination. It is not surprising that the longest segment of Morgan's elaboration is on the issue of organization viewed as the transformation. That is also the metaphor that is most suitable for our radical perspective. That is, the leader should be able to look at the organization from the lens of potential for change. Morgan's taxonomy, however, is not what our radical governing metaphor is about. An organization surely has a dominant perspective which is concentrated in the governing metaphor, but in making radical change we do not have to alter entire organization but just the problematic situation in hand. The problem solving situation can but does not have to be constructed on the same metaphor as a whole organization. The governing metaphor of the decision making situation is certainly embedded in the social construct of the organization, but the metaphor that generates sensemaking of an organization may have peripheral influence on the situation in hand.

So, seen from the contextual perspective, the governing metaphor is the productive character of meaning construction that has a pivotal role in understanding the problem solving as an instance. In a change process, the leader is trying to influence one or more concepts of the organization's mental model. The fundamental issue of change management is whether the concepts are of central or peripheral importance to the creation of meaning.

The governing metaphors of the existing conceptual structures are well known to all people that form the organization. They are referred to as "the way how things are done around here." The leader can address the problem solving situation without trying to change the governing metaphor. By influencing peripheral concepts of the organization's mental model, the leader is only adjusting the sensemaking process while its meaning remains unchanged. On the other hand, the leader can tackle the problem by enacting new governing metaphor, different than the character that formed the *status quo* mental representation. If that is the case, a new meaning of the situation in hand is generated which causes the creation of a radically different mental model of the organization. The governing metaphor which guides the creation of radically new meaning is "the loadstar" of radical decision making process.

Genesis of the loadstar through selective attention

The chapter sets further discussion about the nature of a loadstar around the question of extraction of the loadstar from the flow of experience. First I discuss the place of experience in human understanding, and then I focus on the ways how the stream of experience can be breached in the attempt to extract a concept which will be pivotal in creation of meaning of a problematic instance.

Experience is the primary source of material for construction of meaning. Every concept is an artifact of retrospective. Since experience is placed in the memory, it bears characteristics of this part of human cognitive apparatus. As discussed earlier, the main characteristic of memory is that it is based on the process of construction. This leads us the conclusion how experience, in its meaning construction role, does not have to be something that has happened to us, but that it also might be something we have constructed. Scottish empiricist philosopher David Hume in his book *An Enquiry Concerning Human Understanding* (1974) poses that "the new" is generated by the use of at least four mental operations which produce novel conceptual structures. The operations are compounding (addition of one idea on top of another); transposing (substitution of one part of a thing with the part from another); augmenting; and diminishing. Obviously, he states that a new concept always protrudes from the familiar ones. However, outside of his empiricist approach, Hume (1974, 319) accepts that one can experience a novel idea that itself is derived only from combinations of previous impressions. So, the empirical, sensory apparatus is not the only source of experience. This is why people who made lot of mistakes can harvest the experience and become better decision makers after all.

As noted in the discussion on reflective practice, experience can be viewed as a continuous duration, or as a separate segment. While the process of reflection is based on episodic retrospection, the genesis of a concept that is to become a governing metaphor is based on the process of its extraction from the flow of experience. The concept of flow of experience is derived from the concept of flow of consciousness also posted by James (2006a, 224–229). James, as one of the forefathers of process philosophy, depicts the notion of thought as a continuous flux. The concept poses that the future events are not clear-cut. Fundamentally, the reality is a process of coming into being. Events unfold in a continuous manner and consist out of numerous cause-effect situations that are impossible to predict in a precise manner. This is why a turn of events often looks like a slide down the hill, impossible to stop once it begins to tumble. The notion of reality as a flux opened perspective to a new literary genre: the stream-of-consciousness novel with Marcel Proust and James Joyce as the most well-known exponents of this writing style.

When the novel states of affairs appear, it cracks the stream of consciousness. Whitehead (1997, 125) emphasizes what he calls the atomic character of reality. Actual entities of reality become and perish because of their temporal nature but while they persist they are individualized and become indivisible wholes. As such, the atomic structures can be extracted from the stream and used in the sensemaking process.

Since human understanding is constructed on the basis of one mental schema, one character selected from the overall flow of experience, the question is how this governing concept is extracted. What are the possible ways to find the metaphor that brings radical change? In order to address this question, the genesis of a governing metaphor is observed as the process of selective attention.

Information flow in any real situation is immensely rich. In our vicinity, there are thousands of things we can focus our attention on. The closer we look at an object or event, the more of it we can perceive and learn. The information that is extracted from the overall flow of experience in order to be used in the process of perception is an important part of the research of cognitive decision making process. The cognitive process of selective attention is about concentration on one aspect of the environment and ignoring all other. As James (2007a, 403–404) points out:

> Everyone knows what attention is. It is the taking possession by the mind, in clear and vivid form, of one out of what seem several simultaneously possible objects or trains of thought. Focalization, concentration and consciousness are of the essence. It implies withdrawal from some things in order to deal effectively with the others, and is a condition which has a real opposite in the confused, dazed, scatter-brain state.

The concept of attention, in James's time, at the end of nineteenth century, was considered to be a very important issue by both philosophers and psychologists. Due to the development of behaviorism in the 1920, the concept of attention fell into the background since this research tradition treated all internal processes superficially. Since the 1950s, however, the dominant epistemology of psychology was no longer positivism but realism, so that the exploration of the phenomenon of attention gained importance once again.

An important function of attention for the decision making process is the selection of one part of sensory input for further processing. The fundamental question posed here is how we decide which part of the flow of experience should we concentrate and what consequences this decision has for the available information? There are two options. The first one is that the commitment to one part of the flow of experience over the other is based on the target orientation of the decision maker (Yantis 1993). Selection that is directed to the decision maker's goal reflects the choices we make about the object that we want to pay attention to. Attention is thus closely linked with motivation (Eysenck and Keane 2002; Eysenck 2001). Another approach is that the capacity of attention is automatically overwhelmed with stimuli, regardless of the objectives of the entity (Zimbardo and Gerrig 2002). The first one can be called voluntary attention—the aspect over which we have control and which enables us to act in a goal-directed manner. In contrast, the second one can be referred to as reflexive attention because it is driven by exogenous stimuli which redirect our current focus of attention to a new stimulus (Goldstein 2010, 155–177).

If we selectively pay attention to one part of the perceptual environment, either because of our goals or by the characteristics of the stimuli, one might wonder what is going on with the other available information. This matter was investigated by Donald Broadbent (1958, 297–298), who understood mind as a communication channel, similar to the telephone line, which actively processes and transmits information. According to Broadbent's theory, the mind has limited capacity as a communication channel and therefore cannot execute full information processing. This limitation requires attention to regulating the flow of information from sensory inputs to consciousness. Attention creates a bottleneck in the flow of information through the cognitive system, filtering some information and letting other information pass. Broadbent's filter model is an early selection theory of attention which claims that selection occurs early in the process, before the meaning of inputs is determined. Although conscious memory and object recognition requires our attention, as Broadband explains, very complex information processing goes by the attention and awareness. This stage of information processing occurs on the basis of sensory impulses before they become the subject of attention.

Although it is tempting to consider attention as a filtering process, such a view in the psychological and biological terms is not correct. There is no mechanism, processor or system that regulates the rejection of "unnecessary" information. The decision maker simply does not notice them. Selection is a positive and not a negative process. The decision maker only collects the information for which he can find mental schemata; others are discarded (Neisser 1976, 75). The selective nature of perception is particularly interesting and important in the case where specific mental schemata is present but not used—in one case something is overlooked in the second it is noticed. Those are events of selective attention

Different spin on the issue of selective attention is given by David Kahneman (1973) in his capacity model of attention (Treisman and Kahneman 1984). In the model, attention is described as a resource in which energy or mental effort is required. The more complex the problem solving situations are, the more mental effort demanded from the decision maker. A key component of a successful problem solving is thus allocating enough attention, as a resource, to the task at hand. This is why some authors like Davenport and Beck (2002) pose a thesis that the most significant problem in today's business world is not an uncertain economy or competition but an attention deficit of the decision makers.

As just described, the cognitive process of selective attention has the pivotal role in the process of generation of the loadstar. Before tackling the ways in which the decision maker can extract the governing metaphor from the flow of experience, few more issues concerning the concept of attention in experiencing demand elaboration. First one is that attention mechanisms work in retrospect, the experience is the thing of the past. This notion, according to Weick (1995, 25–26), has a twofold effect: first everything we know about remembering also affects attention and second things that are occurring at the moment influence the things that what will be discovered through retrospect. In this respect, Weick also points out that we cannot know what come first, object of our attention or one of its possible antecedents. This confusing reversal comes about because we can never know what the action means before we have selected the stimulus. The choice of the stimulus and the meaning it brings are primarily influenced by the situational context. For instance, Kahneman and Tversky (1972) note that we will first notice recent events, major changes and dramatic situations. In organizational settings Simon and March (1993, 172–179) emphasize the cognitive dimension of managerial work through the elaboration of the ways in which organizational routines release attention that can be used for non-routine decision making.

Dyer, Gregersen and Christensen (2011, 41–65) point out that a lot of innovation comes back to associative thinking and that, as such, innovation can be a learned skill. One way to get better at the process of selective attention is through mastering the process of abstraction. Abstraction is a thinking process that allows us to deliver our message in a very concise way. The simplicity is achieved by going through many iterations of the problem solving process until we recognize the few most important elements of the solution. The process of achieving abstraction starts with a description of the problem solving embedded in the context. Subsequently, one by one we are removing all elements of the context until only the governing metaphor of the problem solving mental representation remains. Process of abstraction is a fundamental approach to the description of reality in cubist art movement. One of pioneers of the movement Pablo Picasso accounts for this cognitive process in this way (Root-Bernstein and Root-Bernstein 1999, 71–72):

> To arrive at abstraction, it is always necessary to begin with a concrete reality...you must always start with something. Afterward, you can remove all traces of reality. There's no danger then, anyway, because the idea of the object will have left an indelible mark. It is what started the artist off, excited his ideas, and stirred his emotions.

Extracting the governing metaphor, grasping the underlying principles of what's going on through the process of abstraction is not an easy task. It is the point that was made by Jobs in the *Business Week* interview from May 12, 1998: "That's been one of my mantras—focus and simplicity. Simple can be harder than complex: You have to work hard to get your thinking clean to make it simple. But it's worth it in the end because once you get there, you can move mountains." As Jobs has showed, hard work of extraction of the governing metaphor can prove to be quite rewarding.

Of course, genesis of the loadstar does not mean that we will be able to deliver a radical change. There is a difference between imagination and invention, as Stravinsky (1970, 53) points out:

> Invention presupposes imagination but should not be confused with it. For the act of invention implies the necessity of a lucky find and of achieving full realization of this find. What we imagine does not necessarily take on a concrete form and may remain in a virtual state, whereas invention is not conceivable apart from its actual being worked out.

Many companies that came to ground-breaking ideas never utilize them. Steve Jobs puts this well in the 1995 TV show "Triumph of the Nerds" (part III), when he gives a description of his visit to Xerox Parc in December 1979:

And they showed me really three things. But I was so blinded by the first one I didn't even really see the other two... I was so blinded by the first thing they showed me which was the graphical user interface. I thought it was the best thing I'd ever seen in my life. Now remember it was very flawed, what we saw was incomplete, they'd done a bunch of things wrong. But we didn't know that at the time but still though they had the germ of the idea was there and they'd done it very well and within you know ten minutes it was obvious to me that all computers would work like this someday.

The examples like this one happen again and again in business. Apple didn't create the first MP3 player, but it made the most beautiful one. Actually, that is not the case only in business. Far from it. It might come as a surprise that Shakespeare, for instance, borrowed all of his plots down to fine detail, with the exception of "A Midsummer Night's Dream," "Love's Labour's Lost" and "The Tempest," which are wholly original stories (Mabillard, 2000). Even the famed "Copernican revolution," the paradigm shift from the Ptolemaic model of the heaven with a stationary Earth at the center of the universe, was Nicolaus Copernicus's idea. The heliocentric model with the sun at the center of the known universe and with the Earth revolving around it was first presented by Aristarchus of Samos, ancient Greek astronomer and mathematician who lived in third century BC. Also, the contributions to the model were made by Arabic astronomer Averroes in the twelfth century. However, it is in the Copernicus book *De revolutionibus orbium coelestium* (On the revolutions of the celestial spheres) that the heliocentric system was described with detailed diagrams and tables that proved its validity. Construction of mental models is just one part of the game.

Extracting the loadstar from the social context

In order to explain the role of the governing metaphor in the process of radical decision making, it is not enough to explore only the extraction of the loadstar from flow of experience through the process of selective attention, as we did in the last paragraphs. We have to take in consideration the context to which the governing metaphor is to be embedded. Since we deal with organizations, we deal with the most complicated perspective—social context. There are two ways in which we can look at the genesis of the loadstar—it can be either involuntary or deliberate kind of activity.

Although the governing metaphor arises from the process of selective attention which is directed to the decision maker's goal, the decision maker does not have to be actively occupied in trying to breach flow of experience in an attempt to extract the loadstar. This kind of process Starbuck and Milliken (1988) call noticing. Noticing comprises activities of filtering, classifying and comparing. It is informal, involuntary process of metaphor extraction. Attention primarily orients us to the situational or personally primed concepts. In order words, we notice things that are novel, unexpected, extreme, as well as stimuli relevant to our current goals. As Stravinsky (1970, 53) puts it: "In the course of my labors I suddenly stumble upon something unexpected. This unexpected element strikes me. I make a note of it. At the proper time, I put it to profitable use."

On the other hand, the allocation of a governing metaphor from the entire flow of experience sometimes is based on a premeditated process, either on the process of search (Cyert and March 1963) or on the process of scanning (Daft and Weick 1984). Search and especially scanning are more deliberate and hence more under control of preconceptions.

These two ways of extracting cues from flow of experience differ from the perspective of intensity but not from the perspective of consciousness. As such, they are less open to invention than to genesis of the metaphor through the process of noticing. It is so because deliberate search for alternatives is an important but challenging part of the thinking skill set. It acts contrary to the natural tendency of the mind. The natural tendency of the mind refers to determination and arrogance. The goal of a mind is to recognize the situation and take steady action. A multitude of alternatives means that the action is inhibited because the mind finds it discouraging to move simultaneously in the several directions.

In respect to the difference between scanning and noticing we should note that the prerequisite for successful scanning is development of specific "climate" which encourages generation of new solutions. The decision maker can create a context in which it is desirable to actively and systematically search for new solutions. Otherwise, at the organizational level, the search and scanning boils down to noticing.

Besides the organizational effort to encourage searching and scanning as source of novel metaphors that will provide a solution for a problematic instance, there is another way of use of these processes. This process might be called the evolutionary pattern of development of initial mental representations. After the decision maker notices a loadstar through the process of selective attention he can put it in the organizational agenda for confirmation. Members of the top management team then search for clues to confirm the initial loadstar. If the loadstar is confirmed, the entire organization strives for its confirmation by the process of scanning for beneficial cues—the strong identity means that the basic beliefs are often reaffirmed. In other words, search and scanning are processes that we use not only to find new organizational metaphors, but also to confirm metaphor set by the leaders. From that perspective, all organizational activity consists of validating the governing metaphor.

We have showed that the cue extracted as a sense building metaphor primarily depends on the context. Now we will briefly mention another role of the context in genesis of a loadstar—its effect on how the metaphor is interpreted. The meaning of objects or an event cannot be found without a supplied context. In the lack of contextual background, the expressions bare equivocal or multiple meanings. Only within the specific context the interpretation can claim its meaning. That is especially true in the case of social context where it is the usual source of conflicts. From time to time, members of the organization have different interpretations of same events, due to the different contextual embedding they perceive. If the problem situation is such that the interpretation needs to be reconciled across the organization, the difference between interpretations is often the reason for political struggle.

Every decision situation demands a governing metaphor. Decision is a call for action, which emerges in three cases: if an opportunity appears, if there is a threat or if there is a perceived disparity between the desired and the actual state. In each case the quest for a governing metaphor is stimulated by the failure to achieve the goals and continues until an adequate alternative is found. New alternatives are sought in the vicinity of old, and if a failure happens it only focuses the search. The pressure to find an adequate governing metaphor is often very high because the success would allow organizational sensemaking capacity move to other areas. March (1994, 16) explains how this classic system of organizational search and decision making enhances achievement of the objectives in three ways. First, it adjusts performance to the objectives because the decision makers learn about what he should expect. Second, it adapts the performance against objectives through increased efforts in the pursuit in the case of failure and through reduction of efforts in the event of success. Finally, the organizational search for solutions adapts the performance against objectives in one more way—through a reduction of leniency toward poor results and through increase of leniency toward good results.

As just discussed, the loadstar has a twofold role in the leadership process—the task of organizing activities toward the single purpose, and the task of enabler for receiving, noticing and sending information. These two aspects are associated because focused activity opens room for noticing (or rather extracting) elements from the flow of experiences that affirm the governing metaphor.

One of the most important features of a metaphor in the leadership process is giving meaning to the emotional content they bear. Emotions and contradictions that are necessarily embedded in the metaphors can represent a source of motivation for members of the organization as well as an arena which needs to be put in order (which demands sense-making activity) (Nonaka and Yamanouchi 1989, 302). One of the key roles of a leader in implementing the radical decision is to utilize the emotional content of metaphors to instill faith in novel meaning that he strives to enact.

6
Taking a Radical Decision

Abstract: *Hruška examines two connected but separate processes: creation of the radical mental model and the process of its validation—the moment of decision. First, Hruška describes the process of mental model construction which consists of three phases: search for the governing metaphor, construction of initial mental representation and construction of a developed radical mental model. Second, the author deals with the validation of radical mental model. After the radical mental model is constructed and elaborated, the decision maker will find that many aspects are foggy and not accounted for. That is why the leader needs to infuse the mental model with the spirit of hope. Hruška elaborates origins and consequences of the virtue of hope on the radical decision making process.*

Keywords: hope; radical decision taking; validation of radical mental model

Hruška, Domagoj. *Radical Decision Making: Leading Strategic Change in Complex Organizations.*
New York: Palgrave Macmillan, 2015.
DOI: 10.1057/9781137492319.0010.

The die is cast

So far I have posed the problem of creation of a single element which is the seed of new meaning. The governing metaphor leads the decision maker to the creation of the new way of handling the problematic situation. This chapter explores a second step in the process of radical change—after the loadstar is found the leader goes through the process of constructing the radical mental representation. Once the leader has set the radically new mental model it can be validated by deciding to take action based on it. On that line, the chapter consists of two parts—first, the construction and crystallization of the radical mental model and, second, its validation.

Decision taking moment or a defining moment is a point in time when we agree to act accordingly to the mental model we have conceived. The phrase "taking a decision," only refers to the decisive moment itself and not to the process leading up to it that might include research, discussions and so on. The process of preparing the decision as well as the follow-up processes after the decision has been taken in what we call the decision making process. In the first segment of the chapter, we will explore the psychology of the defining moments in radical decision situations through the insights from the famous historical event—invasion of Rome by Julius Caesar in 49 BC.

Alea iacta est—the die is cast is a well-known Latin phrase attributed to Julius Caesar, which he said on January 10, 49 BC as he led his army across the river Rubicon in northern Italy. The phrase describes perhaps the most celebrated turning point recorded in history—a moment of radical decision taking.

Gaius Julius Caesar was born in 100 BC into a patrician family. Although his father died when he was sixteen, Caesar managed to advance through the military and political structures of the Empire rising to the rank of praetor, an important political post. At first Caesar began to align with Pompey, young but already famous military commander, who proved to be a competent leader and gifted strategist. Caesar also cultivated his political partnership with Crassus, who is cited as the wealthiest man in Roman history. In 60 BC, Caesar, Crassus and Pompey formed a political alliance that dominated Roman politics for several years. At a conference in Luca in 56 BC the three leaders cemented Caesar's existing territorial rule of Gaul (now France and Belgium) for another five years, and approved Crassus a five-year term in Syria and Pompey a five-year term in Spain. Things went well between the men in the triumvirate, at first; in fact, Pompey married Julia, Caesar's daughter. Three years later, however, Crassus was killed in a battle in Syria. With the Gallic Wars concluded, the Senate called upon Caesar to leave his command and disband his army or risk being acknowledged an "enemy of the state." Pompey was entrusted with enforcing this edict.

What will follow is a greatest Roman civil war. The evidence of these events is a rare example of a first-hand historical account of major events written by the major protagonist. Not many people know that besides being a general and politician, Caesar was also an outstanding writer. In his work "The Commentaries" Caesar (2007a, b) gives account of the events that follow his rise to power. The described events are divided in two parts, first half of which appears as the story of conquest of Gaul, and the second part concerns the time from the passage of the Rubicon in January 49 BC to Pompey's death and the start of the Alexandrian War in the autumn of the subsequent year. In the concluding half of Caesar's Commentaries, the narrated events are concerned with his vain efforts in trying to get Pompey to accede to the peace in order to avert a conflict. Although Caesar's story focuses on the military events, there are some, though limited, references to the political side of events.

In a nutshell—Caesar refused the Senate's order and goes to war against Pompey. By the end of 48 BC, Caesar had pushed his enemies out of Italy and pursued Pompey into Egypt, where he was ultimately killed.

On that January 10 of 49 BC Caesar had a decision to make. Either he complies with the Senate's command or he moves southward to confront Pompey and throw the Roman Republic into a violent civil war. An ancient Roman law forbade any general from passing the Rubicon River with a standing army. This tiny stream would disclose Caesar's intents and mark the point of no return.

As noted, the background of the story, stating the reasons of the great political changes which will seal the fall of the Republic, is given by Caesar himself. However, the decisive moment on the Rubicon were described in detail by Suetonius, a Roman historian and biographer who had access to the privileged imperial documents and correspondence upon which he based his accounts. In his work "Lives of the Twelve Caesars," Suetonius focused more on their personal conduct and habits than on public events.

The defining moment at the Rubicon determined all subsequent related events. Suetonius (1889, 31) says:

> Coming up with his troops on the banks of the Rubicon, which was the boundary of his province, he halted for a while, and, revolving in his mind the importance of the step he was on the point of taking, he turned to those about him, and said: We may still retreat; but if we pass this little bridge, nothing is left for us but to fight it out in arms.

Caesar and his armies hesitate rather long at this river while he decides what to do. He is conscious that he's risking not just his life, but those of his loyal soldiers and that he might not win. Once the dice start rolling they cannot be stopped. This was Caesars defining moment. The same kind of defining moment eventually every one of us has to face. Everything that happened before in our lives led us to this moment. While Caesar reflects, let us wait with him; feel his anxiety; imagine the turmoil of the numerous thoughts in his head.

Suetonius (1889, 32) continues his account:

> While he was thus hesitating, the following incident occurred. A person remarkable for his noble mien and graceful aspect appeared close at hand, sitting and playing upon a pipe. When, not only the shepherds, but a number of soldiers also flocked from their posts to listen to him, and some trumpeters among them, he snatched a trumpet from one of them, ran to the river with it, and sounding the advance with a piercing blast, crossed to the other side.

We do not know who the person with the trumpet is, this is the only instance we hear of him. However, his appearance is not a miracle. He was there; he knew Caesar's situation and his thinking. He ignited the first flame because he believed in Caesar's leadership.

"Upon this, Caesar exclaimed, 'Let us go whither the omens of the Gods and the iniquity of our enemies call us. *The die is now cast*'" (Suetonius, 1889, 33). So he takes a decision, uses the famous gambling metaphor, crosses the river and changes world's history.

Construction of the radical mental model

In the last chapter, we got familiar with the process of extraction of the loadstar from the flow of experience. In order to construct mental models, we need to embed the governing metaphor in *status quo* conceptual structure.

Construction of the radical mental representation arises from the interaction of decision makers governing metaphor, the loadstar, with the elements of the environment. In order to be successful in this process, the leader needs to have good insight of the contextual variables. The insight is gained through the process of reflection on experience. Steve Jobs puts this issue in an interesting way in an interview in *Wired* magazine of February 1996:

> Creativity is just connecting things. When you ask creative people how they did something, they feel a little guilty because they didn't really do it, they just saw something. It seemed obvious to them after a while. That's because they were able to connect experiences they've had and synthesize new things. And the reason they were able to do that was that they've had more experiences, or they have thought more about their experiences than other people.

In general, there are two ways to look at construction of new conceptual structures. First one is that we look at it in terms of spontaneous generation, by the stroke of inspired genius. Second one is to see it as an evolutionary process.

The functioning of old theories as metaphors for new situations is essential for both perspectives. As argued, new concepts do not spring from anything; they come from old ones. They emerge out of the interaction of old concepts and new situations. The process Schön (1963, 192) calls "displacement of concepts": "a process in which old concepts, in order to function as projective models for new situation, come themselves to be seen in new ways." Radical quality of the process is in the fact that the old concept is not simply reapplied unchanged to the new situation but is seen in the light of the new instance.

Construction of a radical mental representation in both cases, in inspirational and evolutionary case, is based on the interpretation of new stimuli in respect to already present mental schemata. New inputs modify the existing mental model which is in turn used to gather more information. The cycle is repeated until the action ultimately results with the mental representation of the situation that the leader can confirm as the basis for the activities of implementation of the mental representations in reality.

Inspirational and evolutionary modes of radical mental models construction differ from two perspectives—pace of construction and needed decision maker's effort. In contrast to the inspirational mode, the evolutionary approach does not happen in one moment but it requires numerous linkages in the chain of events that are leading the decision maker to the solution. The mental model of the situation was the object of discovery over a period and glimpse of its current shape where available for observation and experiments. Evolutionary construction is an active process of the incremental nature while the radical mental construction in the inspiration mode is generated instantly and without much effort.

In both cases, the process of construction of radical mental models is based on three phases: a loadstar, construction of initial mental representation and construction of elaborated radical mental model.

In its earliest form, in the form of metaphors, mental models largely involve emotions as well as the elements that have been forgotten or unconsciously perceived (Polanyi 1969, 185–192). In the absence of a better term, this phase of the development of mental models might be called "intuition." In this stage of the mental model development, the intuitive belief is not verbally articulated.

The mental representation of the decision problem can be self-explanatory, with the low level of uncertainty, especially if the problem in hand is common and well known. In such situations, the leader can make a swift decision. Radical decisions are never of such quality. The direction of construction of mental representation, embedded in the loadstar, attracts contextual variables and builds the initial mental model of a radical decision. In the process of implementation of radical change, the leader's mental representation will undoubtedly be changed by the activity of members of the organization who must act in accordance with it. In that way, from the leader's initial radical mental model, mental models of each member of the organization are derived. These derived radical mental models confirm the governing metaphor of the initial model through actions of all organizational members.

The initial mental model of radically changed situation is vague and ambiguous. It is an initial embedding of the governing metaphor in concrete decision making context. The development of the initial concept into the final construction which is ready to be validated depends upon the number of conditions that must be met. Three kinds of conditions bear pivotal importance in the process—emotional, rational and intuitive prerequisites. Initial mental model is tested in respect to these three issues.

Emotional test regards the belief in the correctness of the decisions in hand. It is a question of whether the initial mental model corresponds to the "heart" of the decision maker. Rational confirmation is based on getting to know the context of the decision making process in order to determine all possible scenarios of the decision. The initial radical mental model will pass the test if the decision maker can accept consequences of the worst case scenario.

The third test is what I call the "intuitive test." It corresponds to the "gut feeling" of the decision maker. It is the: "does it feel right?" issue. Principally, this test is based on trust in the people involved in the process of the implementation of the decision. As Steve Jobs puts it in the *Rolling Stone* magazine June 16, 1994, interview:

> Technology is nothing. What's important is that you have faith in people, that they're good and smart, and if you give them tools, they'll do wonderful things with them. It's not the tools that you have faith in—tools are just tools. They work, or they don't work. It's people you have faith in or not. Yeah, sure, I'm still optimistic I mean, I get pessimistic sometimes but not for long.

If the initial mental representation of radical decision situation passes the three crucial tests the process of construction of radical mental model is finished. Such, elaborated, mental model becomes the object of final validation by the decision maker.

Validation of the radical mental model

A defining moment is the moment of validation of elaborated mental representation. To validate the radical decision means to accept the radically altered mental model as a base for the activities that lead to radical change.

The process of radical decisions making differs from the classic decision making process primarily on this question. While the classical theory deals with the selection of one of the numerous options in decision maker's strategic arena, the model of radical decision making assumes that the decision maker has only one option. It is not unusual, however, that the organizational dynamics yields with the situation in which a decision making situation is based on only one available alternative. In these instances the set of options is not necessarily unavailable but is unthinkable even when it is available. The decision makers cannot imagine options due to the institutional residue of previous political activities and their impact on the distribution of authority and knowledge throughout the organization (Salancik and Copper Brindle 1997,

115–116). Existence of the single alternative in radical decision making is of the different nature.

After construction of the radical mental representation, the decision maker is considering whether it can be carried out, but not whether he should choose another radical approach. For the radical decision is a question of whether the leader should try to change the meaning of the decision making situation. In other words, in radical decision making problem of choice is of binary nature—the radical mental model is either confirmed or not. The decision is based on the acceptance of the radical path.

Validation of radical decisions cannot be interpreted by the satisfying behavior as described by Simon (1997, 118–120). Research on a satisfying level of decision maker's aspiration deals with triggers by which the search for new alternatives initiates and ends. This optimization issue is the problem of balancing the expected costs of additional search with the expected benefits that can be realized through a new option (March and Simon 1993, 161–162). From this perspective validation of the radical mental model is based on a comparison of *status quo* situation and the situation after the novel meaning is established. The new situation is certainly more satisfying, but the leader has to take in the consideration possibility of falling short in the implementation and the consequences that such turn of events will bring about.

Validation of a radical decision is in principle the question of accepting radically altered mental model as an origin of activities that lead to radical changes. As a simplified representation of reality, mental models will always be incomplete and imprecise. In a complex organizational environment, it is impossible to make precise causal relationships. Radical decision makers operate within the unorganized system and try to establish a new order in a world that is perceived as open to influences and shaped through numerous iterations of thinking and action. In this kind of process, the key role in the validation of radical mental model is the ability to believe that most of uncounted for variables will turn out to our advantage. In other words, it is a question of hope.

Hope as the antidote for fear

We did all we can. We elaborated the novel representation to the fullest level possible, explored all possible segments of the novel situation and prepared ourselves to all opposition that we will face. But that is just not enough. Simply too many obstacles cannot be predicted, and change of people's minds is notoriously hard to take for granted. So many crucial issues are foggy and impossible to predict. We need something more that our *ratio* can offer. We need to infuse the radical mental model with the spirit of hope.

Our lives are "experimental lives," as Ulrich Beck (1992, 36) says. Mediated and stereotypical roles in society are not effective anymore. Today, we do not lead the life given to us at birth, but the life that we create for ourselves. In earlier times it was normal that a family member will continue the craft that his family passed down from generation to generation. Lamarck in his hypothesis of inheritance of acquired characteristics has even claimed that such a practice is justified by hereditary characteristics—carpenter's son will be a good carpenter. Today, that continuity is broken. All call for openness, freedom, the possibility of human self-realization. Jung (1983) therefore explains life through the process of man's constant confrontation with the world—on one hand the confrontation with the expected norms and values, and on the other hand with the internal requirements of the psyche that are manifested in longings and dreams.

Postmodern freedom of creating one's own life has its dark side. If the maxim is that every man and woman is the artisan of his own fortune, then we are also responsible for the misfortune. Almost everything in life depends on the decisions that we make ourselves. However, man is unable to respond simultaneously to all decisions in an adequate manner. We will inevitably have to cope with a situation that entails fear. A man is seized by fear when he suddenly finds himself confronted by a complex, equivocal situation in which he feels helpless and thinks that he is unable to respond to it in a satisfactory manner.

The fewer the rules that are restricting our choices, the more "free" we are and the more the fear that permeates our lives. It is necessary, therefore, to know how to productively deal with fear. A man can be freed from fear only if he competently relates to the present and can confidently look to the future that will bring predictable changes. In other words, the radical leader has to master the virtue of hope.

Hope is "the virtue of the energetic entrepreneur who seeks a future, difficult, but attainable good" as McClosky (2006, 160) calls it citing Aquinas. First and foremost, hope is a virtue. The word "virtue" in today's language has lost much of its meaning. To understand it well we must bear in mind its etymological meaning—in Latin *virtus* means "strength." Four virtues play a pivotal role in human life and accordingly are called "cardinal." In one form or another, these virtues have been revisited in many places and instances, from Babylonian plains, over Greek city-states to Japanese "military school road." The most famous elaboration of the cardinal virtues are discussed by Plato (2008) in *The Republic* as well as by Aristotle who elaborated his theory of virtue in two texts, the *Nicomachean Ethics* (1893) and the *Eudemian Ethics* (1868). The cardinal virtues are: prudence, justice, fortitude and temperance. Prudence is called *auriga virtutum*—the charioteer of the virtues as it guides our actions in accordance with the judgment of conscience. The prudent man determines and directs his conduct with this judgment. As St. Thomas Aquinas (SS, QQ[47], 2), following Aristotle, writes— prudence is "right reason applied to action". Justice is the virtue that consists in the steady and firm will to make sure that everyone gets what he is entitled to. Temperance ensures the will's mastery over instincts. Fortitude ensures firmness in difficulties and reliability in our pursuits. Aquinas recognizes the same four cardinal virtues. However, he thinks that to understand human nature fully, we must consider redeemed human nature. Redemption equips us for union with God by infusing us with the theological virtues of faith, hope and charity—faith refers to believe in God and all that he has revealed; hope places trust in Christ's promises; and charity enables us to love God for his own sake and our neighbor as ourselves for the love of God. According to Christian teaching, theological virtues infuse and elevate our natural virtues.

Hope is, therefore, a matter of trust. As Aquinas puts it: "[T]he object of hope is a future good, difficult but possible to obtain" (SS, QQ[17], 1). Hope is not some vague, hazy and distant feeling, but a confidence in what we do. Not the trust in ourselves, nor in the human calculations or combinations but in the correctness of the goals that we want to achieve. It is a certainty through which man gets great strength.

Hope is grounded in identity. In order to be a virtue, to represent strength, hope should have a well-built foundation; it should rely on the truth. Faith provides this foundation of hope—the identity of the decision maker and of the organization. In order to make and implement radical decision, the leader must be convinced that his perspective is the only way in which the organization should be developed. In other words, he has to have faith.

The question of origins of hope is a major difference between the use of the word in Aristotle's and Christian system. Aristotle treats the word as a possibility of both, doing good and doing evil. The Greek term typically interpreted as hope in the New Testament is *elpis*. In the New Testament context, the word implies "hope for good things" (Rom. 8:24). In Aristotle, however, the term *elpis* plays a more neutral position, being the rough equivalent of the looking forward to the future or better anticipate or expect (Gravlee 2000, 461–462).

By contrast of faith, hope is forward looking. Hope can only exist in people who have not yet attained the goals they seek. It is, thus, constantly concerned with something in the future. Hope is also what we can call an entrance to faith in the sense that it is the entrance to the thing believed since by hope we enter in to see what it is that we believe. Radical decisions are a matter of construction of the new identity, made from the governing metaphor upon which we bestow our hopes.

According to Aquinas (SS, QQ[17], 4) hope refers to two things, namely,

> the good which it intends to obtain, and the help by which that good is obtained. Now the good which a man hopes to obtain, has the aspect of a final cause, while the help by which one hopes to obtain that good, has the character of an efficient cause. Now in each of these kinds of cause we find a principal and a secondary cause. For the principal end is the last end, while the secondary end is that which is referred to an end.

The "final cause" in the radical decision making refers to the governing metaphor that we want to establish through the process of radical change, using different means—the "efficient" causes.

Juxtapositioning hope with fear goes all the way back to Aquinas:

> Just as hope has two objects, one of which is the future good itself, that one expects to obtain, while the other is someone's help, through whom one expects to obtain what one hopes for, so, too, fear may have two objects, one of which is the very evil which a man shrinks from, while the other is that from which the evil may come. (SS, QQ[18], 1)

Hope heals us from fear and discouragement. Hope is stronger that fear. This stream of thinking is complementary with Aristotle's thesis that hope is most intimately connected with courage (Gravlee 2000, 469–470). If hope weakens, man is closing in his selfish strategies marked by fear. Hope is like a source that continually cleanses the heart and gives, beyond fatigue and lukewarmness, a new youthful vigor.

Hope is a matter of will, a choice that often demands effort. It is easier to be worried, discouraged and afraid. To hope is to have the confidence, to believe. That expression shows how hope is not about being passive but about performing an act. "To give up" or "to lose" hope are often heard expressions. They ordinarily mean that some good thing is beyond our reach. Due to the failure, disappointment, difficulty, through the experience of its misery, because of concern that consume us, we lose energy and eventually give up. Remedy against all that is not an effort of will but the awakening of hope, finding of new confidence in the goal that we want to achieve and in the actions that we can undertake. Appropriate treatment lies in detecting the root of discouragement, "the point of despair," and to adopt a specific remedy that basically consists in the fact that this particular aspect of our undertaking is looked upon with hope. This corresponds to a simple but important psychological reality of life—in order for our will to be strong and enterprising it should be driven by the desire. The desire will be strong only if that what is desired seems to be reachable. If we imagine something as elusive, it ceases to be strongly desired. In other words, we cannot effectively desire something if we psychologically feel that we will never get it. When the will weakens, in order to wake it up, we should redefine our notions. That will allow us to see our goal once again as reachable and desirable.

Similar kind of question is posed in a situation of collapse of the sensemaking structures caused by the outside factors like an accident or natural disaster. Possibility of finding a new meaning is necessary for survival. This question is prompted by Lear's (2008) philosophical and ethical inquiry of how should one face the possibility that one's culture might collapse. Lear uses the anthropology and history of the Indian tribes for the duration of their incarceration to reservations, specifically the story of the Crow Nation. The collapse of the enacted meaning of the Crow Nation is best put in the words of the last great chief—Plenty Coups (Lear 2008, 2): "When the buffalo went away the hearts of my people fell to the ground, and they could not lift them up again. After this nothing happened." Lear discusses the way how societies—and especially the individuals who lead them—carry on when key concepts of their culture become obsolete. In other words—when the meaning of their enactment changes. To one's survival of such situation hope is the core virtue, the courage to hope for the future good that cannot yet be conceived. That is exactly the point of the defining moment in radical decision making—being able to hope for the world created by the new metaphor.

Hope is a critical part of solving any managerial problem of strategic quality. Fundamentally, it is the belief that something is possible and probable. However, it cannot be reduced to a mechanical prediction in the style of positivism. Hope is not about taking risk. It is notable oddity of charlatans to think how they have the information to make accurate judgments about future in every case.

We do not have the precise map of where we are going, but we have a strong feeling that we are called to get there. If we act in confidence, grounded in our identity, the advantageous opportunities will open in our strategic space at every instance of the way. Being able to instill hope is one of the most important leadership traits. Giving employees and teams a clear message of hope, ability to believe in novel mental metaphor, results in both purpose and profit.

7
Rhetoric of Radical Change

Abstract: *Hruška gives practical insight into the ways of persuasion. First, the author explores people's resistance to change the* status quo *mental models. Particular attention is given to the leader's role in the process of reducing resistance to change in radical decision making situations. Also, Hruška explores rhetoric based on beliefs as argumentation and expectation setting and rhetoric based on action as behavioral commitment and manipulation. The author also gives particular attention to the description of the three phases of the incremental process of rhetoric for radical change. Finally, Hruška describes a* parrhesian *approach to radical rhetoric, which in his opinion, is the most suitable way of persuasion in radical change situations.*

Keywords: argumentation; behavioral commitment; expectation setting; manipulation; *parrhesia*; resistance to change

Hruška, Domagoj. *Radical Decision Making: Leading Strategic Change in Complex Organizations.*
New York: Palgrave Macmillan, 2015.
DOI: 10.1057/9781137492319.0011.

The rhetoric of liberty

Driving from the Aristotle's (2010, 6) definition of rhetoric as "the ability, in each particular case, to see the available means of persuasion," the introductory part of the chapter discusses the importance of rhetoric in leadership. We examine the lessons from Abraham Lincoln's art of persuasion amid the intense political and moral debates that absorbed America during the late 1950s, especially the disagreement over slavery and its development that culminated in the Civil War.

Abraham Lincoln was the president of the United States during its most perilous period. He enabled the emancipation of slaves and preserved the Union during the Civil War. Lincoln was assassinated in 1865, days after his second inauguration to the office. Lincoln's rhetorical greatness is well known, so many people are under the false notion that Lincoln was always a skilled public communicator. That is, however, far from the truth. His life is an interesting story of the rise from modest beginnings to achieve the highest office in the country. Born in Kentucky and raised in Indiana, his formal education was modest, to say the least; an estimated total of 18 months—a few days or weeks at a time.

There are many occasions in Lincoln's career that might be a good case for discussion about rhetoric: the famed Gettysburg address or one of the probably most overlooked statements of his presidency—the text to Congress which he called back into special session on July 4, 1861—a rousing and politically savvy call to arms against the Confederacy or his well-known second Inaugural Address, to name just a few. I will focus on one rhetoric episode which is probably the most radical one—the series of debates with Senator Steven Douglas on the issue of slavery.

The Lincoln–Douglas Debates of 1858 were a sequence of seven debates, held in seven towns in the state of Illinois from August 21 to October 15, between Abraham Lincoln, then the Republican candidate, and Senator Stephen Douglas, the Democratic Party candidate for the Senate in Illinois. The debates were the most significant moments in Lincoln's career from the position of public persuasion.

The main topic of the Lincoln–Douglas Debates was slavery—an issue of huge importance to citizens across the nation. Douglas defended the generally accepted, and in 1854 legally enacted, doctrine of so-called popular sovereignty, which meant that the people on the territories of Kansas and Nebraska could decide for themselves whether or not to allow slavery. Lincoln, on the other hand, took at that time a radical position that the "popular sovereignty" would perpetuate slavery and raise it to the national level. He claimed that slavery was not only the deprivation of African Americans but also the broader oppression of social hierarchy.

The difference between Lincoln and Douglas was diametric in their stands but also in their backgrounds. Bordewich illustrates the point in the paper published in *Smithsonian Magazine* in September 2008 with the remark that "Lincoln, whose campaign funds were limited, traveled modestly by coach. Douglas rolled along in style, ensconced in his own private railway car, trailed by a flatcar fitted with a cannon dubbed 'Little Doug,' which fired off a round whenever the train approached a town."

Never before had an incumbent senator agreed to debate his challenger in public so that the public excitement ran high. At first Lincoln was on the defensive but unlike Douglas, who always offered the same arguments, Lincoln was always looking for a new viewpoint to use. Lincoln navigated the limitations posed by his audiences and situations, and he took advantage of creative opportunities. His rhetoric was about impact and momentum, and it had significant tactical quality. By the fourth debate, at Charleston, the public's opinion started to shift.

Lincoln thought deeply on the subject of liberty; in Peoria he powerfully stated that:

> Little by little, but steadily as men march to the grave, we have been giving up the old for the new faith. Nearly eighty years ago we began by declaring that all men are created equal; but now from that beginning we have run down to the other declaration, that for some men to enslave others is a "sacred right of self-government." These principles cannot stand together. They are as opposite as God and Mammon; and whoever holds to the one must despise the other. (Basler 1989, 275)

At the next debate, in Galesburg, estimates of the crowd ranged up to 25,000. Lincoln successfully used his ability of public persuasion to create a sense of community with the audience and to influence his listeners to accomplish his goals. Lincoln's punch line was to challenge Douglas's racism on moral grounds (Basler and Sandburg 2008, 193):

> I suppose that the real difference between Judge Douglas and his friends, and the Republicans on the contrary, is that the Judge is not in favor of making any difference between slavery and liberty... and consequently every sentiment he utters discards the idea that there is any wrong in slavery. Judge Douglas declares that if any community wants slavery, they have a right to have it. He

can say that, logically, if he says that there is no wrong in slavery; but if you admit that there is a wrong in it, he cannot logically say that anybody has a right to do wrong.

With this argument, Lincoln managed to rise above the conventional racism of his time. From his position, liberty was the cornerstone of the Republic, enshrined in Declaration of Independence which he used as a reference point for his position. In the last debate in Alton, Lincoln famously asserted that the authors of the Declaration of Independence

> intended to include all men, but they did not mean to declare all men equal in all respects. They did not mean to say all men were equal in color, size, intellect, moral development or social capacity. They defined with tolerable distinctness in what they did consider all men created equal—equal in certain inalienable rights, among which are life, liberty, and the pursuit of happiness... They meant to set up a standard maxim for free society which should be familiar to all: constantly looked to, constantly labored for, and even, though never perfectly attained, constantly approximated, and thereby constantly spreading and deepening its influence and augmenting the happiness and value of life to all people, of all colors, everywhere. (Ball 2012, 71)

Although Lincoln's argumentation seems perfectly sound to us, as we are aware of the immorality of slavery, we have to keep in mind that Douglas was debating in favor of a large part to the past, in which slavery seemed reasonable and defensible. Lincoln's arguments were sound but also radical.

While Lincoln may have won the debates, he lost the election. On Election Day, the Democrats won, and the new legislature would re-elect Douglas 54 percent to 46 percent. After losing the election, Lincoln edited the texts of all the debates and had them published in a book. The widespread media coverage of the debates and the consequent popularity of the book greatly raised Lincoln's national profile and led eventually to his nomination for the president of the United States in 1860. As it often happens with radical endeavors, even if we are not successful in the first attempt, the change can still happen.

Lincoln's experience shows us the importance of thinking rhetorically, reckoning with specific audiences and situations in mind. In this case, combination of lawyerly logic with evangelical zeal to achieve several daunting, but essential goals proved to be winning the combination. Lincoln's rhetoric is an illustration of lucidity, bluntness of diction, candor, declarative interrogatories, seizing the rhetorical initiative and maintaining argumentative impetus. However, it was more than that. In his eulogy to his role model statesman Henry Clay, Lincoln wrote that Clay's eloquence did not result from the use of rhetorical devices but rather from the "impassioned tone" that comes from deep conviction (Wilson 2013, 15). With Lincoln writings in our hands, we can say the same for him.

Holding on to the *status quo*

Implementation of any change is about fighting old ways and structures. It is a fact of life that many good ideas are never implemented in practice. Most important reason for that is that new initiatives are often in conflict with the existing mental models. Since the radical change is about altering the existing system of values and meanings that shape models of cognition and action, the leader's role is to challenge existing assumptions enacted in the organization, without causing people's overpowering defensive reactions.

Many good ideas are never put into practice. Senge (1990, 14) asserts that one reason for this is that the new approaches and initiatives often conflict with the existing mental models. The task of the decision maker is to challenge existing assumptions, described by the concept of enacted situation, without causing defensive reaction from other organizational agents. This is why, in implementing radical decisions, the leader should use a different approach to each member of the organization, depending on the impact that a person has on the formation of organizational enactment. The clash of interpretations that causes suboptimal organizational performance is well illustrated by Steve Jobs in the *Time Magazine* interview from October 16, 2005:

> You know how you see a show car, and it's really cool, and then four years later you see the production car, and it sucks? And you go—What happened? They had it! They had it in the palm of their hands! They grabbed defeat from the jaws of victory! What happened was, the designers came up with this great idea. Then they take it to the engineers, and the engineers go, "Nah, we can't do that. That's impossible." And so it gets a lot worse. Then they take it to the manufacturing people, and they go, "We can't build that!" And it gets a lot worse.

Implementation and construction of radical mental representations are interdependent in the sense that it is doubtful whether the decision maker is able to construct a mental model for which he in advance knows that it cannot be accomplished. The issue was at the center of attention when we discussed the theme of hope in the last chapter.

In everyday's coping with the world, the decision maker generates certain expectations that are the result of existing concepts that are constantly upgraded. Experience shapes concepts, patterns and structures. As a rule, we follow the established pattern. Researchers at Harvard Medical School came to the conclusion that 60–80 percent of adults find the task of thinking different uncomfortable, and some even find it exhausting (Carson 2010). In order to be efficient, the diagnostic frameworks we use have to be very flexible, open and choice-based rather than prescriptive. Most people, however, deal with the problematic situation with the prescription in mind—knowing in advance how to fix it. As we have argued in the chapter about building mental models for effective leadership, in order to advance, it is necessary to retrospectively search for experience and learn from it. We do not have well-developed mechanisms for such retrospective search or change of patterns. Progress is, therefore, slow.

After we have solved the problem, once we have found a way of dealing with it, we have a strong impulse to stick with the solution. Our mental apparatus operates under imperative of "do not change what is good enough." However, as Heraclitus remarks, the only thing that is constant is change. Some concepts might have longer duration than the others, but over time they will also develop, grow and become more mature and at some stage move into new concepts in a constant process of change (Kuhn 2002; Schumpeter 1934). The formulation of radically new mental model, however, always requires us to break these settled ways of looking at things. Formal models that are readily taken as the truth can freeze the organizational agent's perception of the world and the result in a sort of strategic myopia (Mason and Mitroff 1981; Morgan 1980). Cognitive stability may result with the impossibility of implementing organizational change (Barr, Stimpert and Huff 1992). Therefore, companies or industries that are influenced by cognitive stability represent an opportunity for the introduction of radically new metaphors and mental models, the process that Schumpeter (1934, 16) calls the creative destruction.

Rhetorical perspective on leadership offers a realistic and useful means for understanding how leaders emerge, how they maintain their power and how they build effective, cohesive groups. By knowing how best to construct an argument that resonates at both an intellectual and emotional level, aspiring leaders develop the rhetorical skills critical to their success. Wood (2007, 15–16) asserts that a rhetorical perspective on leadership is characterized by two features: (1) the persuasive nature of the leading process and (2) the recognition that humans can control their environments by adapting to social circumstances. Both issues are of big importance in radical decision making.

Decisions are made by individuals, but always in cooperation with the others, and always with the idea that they will need to be implemented, understood or approved by others. For this reason, a set of considerations that is taken into account in a decision situation should be shared by others and acceptable to them. The answer to the question of how we can achieve organizational change in such an interdependent context can be found in consideration of Lewin's (1951) field theory of social change. Lewin defined a social "field" consisting of the collective, its elements and environment and suggested that the main cause of resistance to social change is in individuals' beliefs in the value of existing social norms. To cause organizational change, therefore, one cannot focus entirely on the level of the collective, nor at the individual level. The focus should be on the interface between the two—the value that individuals place on the norms of the collective. The approach gives significant insight to the implementation of radical decisions because it suggests the focus of effort in the rhetoric process. Powerful leadership tools in this respect provide the discipline of organizational narratives (Czarniawska 1997, 1998; Denning 2004, 2007).

Resistance to change depends on the rhetoric of the leader but also on several contextual variables. Four such factors bear most importance in radical decision making. Two of them lower the resistance to change and other two increase it. Resistance to change is reduced in the case of an unstable context and in the case when the leader projects a high level of confidence on his followers. In the case of low level of people's adeptness and poor interpersonal relations, the resistance to change is increased.

The similar approach is argued by Lewin (1951, 53–54) in the thesis that social change can be achieved most successfully if one first decreases the tension between the opposing forces. The tension reduction "unfreezes" enacted meaning, in Lewin's vocabulary "collective norms" around which the opposing forces have stabilized. The next steps are to transform the enacted meaning to the state of the leader's radical representation and finally to "re-freeze" in a radical state.

Belief-driven rhetoric as arguing and expecting

Rhetoric is any persuasion resulting from human interaction, achieved in other ways than by force or threat. Rhetorical sensitivity to the methods of persuasion can enhance most people's abilities to lead well.

Although the processes of social construction of meaning are ambiguous and difficult to describe, it can be said that there are basically two ways in which the leader can influence people in the organization to combine elements of the flow of experience with contextual framework in the interest of meaning. The influence can start as a belief or as an activity-driven process. The structures of belief and action are described by Weick (1995, 133–169) as the sensemaking triggers. I argue, however, that the beliefs and actions can also be used as sensegiving tools in driving the implementation of change.

Beliefs serve as an anchor which perpetuates future events, including the action and the subsequent beliefs. Beliefs are incorporated into the frameworks such as ideologies or paradigms which influence the way in which people perceive events and consequently react on them. Weick (1995, 134) describes our working set of beliefs as the system of selective perception. Rhetoric based on beliefs can take the form of argumentation or form of expectation setting. In the case of arguments the relationship suggests contradiction, whereas in the case of setting expectations the relationship is based on confirmation.

When we think about rhetoric, we, usually, think only about argumentation. The word "argument" has both social and individual meaning (Billig 1989, 44–45). Individual meaning refers to the part of the discourse that is the point of debate. Social meaning argument applies to disputes between individuals aimed to the solution of the conflict. Cohen, March and Olsen (1972, 25) had illustrated the point well when they defined organizational sensemaking as a set of procedures for argumentation and interpretation as well as problem solving and decision making. The tool of influence in argumentation is language. Therefore, most of the argumentation in organizations takes place at meetings. Meetings are the form that creates and maintains the organization as an entity through enabling members of the organization to come to activities and find meaning in these activities as well as a sense of their relationships (Schwartzman 1989, 288). Meetings thus define, present and reproduce social entities as well as relationships.

In addition to argumentation, beliefs can be the basis of a radical decision maker's rhetoric in another way—when they are blended in expectations that influence the interpretation of the observed events. Weick (1995, 145) argues that in comparison with the arguments, expectations have a more powerful effect on the organizational agents. The main reason for this is that expectations can be a source of inaccuracies in the search for meaning because they act as filters for incoming data— the attention. Expectations of a particular stimulus direct the decision maker to a recognition of the stimulus despite the fact that the actual stimulus is only similar to the expected one. Setting expectations is very good rhetorical mechanism for radical decision making because it is very flexible. Namely, if the event differs from expectations, both can be customized to fit the purpose.

Action-driven rhetoric as committing and manipulating

The rhetoric of implementation of radical decisions can arise from a focus on what people do, not only from what they believe in. Indeed, the search for meaning, usually, starts with action, not beliefs. Members of the organization cannot ignore the activities because they are responsible for them. Activities can be the basis of search for meaning based on the same premise that we described for the rhetoric of arguments and expectations. As we discussed in numerous instances so far, it is linked between beliefs and actions what defines the conceptual framework of search for meaning as an adequate tool for depicting organizational complexity. Such a structure of mutual causality negates the language of casualty in describing social phenomena.

Rhetoric of actions is based on institutional power. There are two basic types of power in the organizational context—power of argumentation and institutional power (Salancik and Copper Brindle 1997, 111). The power of arguments, as well as the argument of power, usually ends up as a disappointment for one side, what raises the question of legitimacy. On the other hand, power can be displayed through the institutionalization of the rules that are to be obeyed in a particular social context. Institutional power is of fundamental importance to the stability of decision making in organizations. Institutional power is the most plausible kind of power, and it exists in most organizations. Those who are affected by the institutional power almost do not notice it. Institutional power is expressed through the rules and policies that form the roles of all members of the organization, and thus determine who has the right to make or authorize decisions. Such relations define interdependence that determines which options will have more importance in the decision making situation and ultimately shape the behavior of organizational agents. In other words, how the change will be implemented.

Rhetoric based on action can take two forms: behavioral commitment and manipulation. First one starts with action for which the person is responsible and the second starts with action that causes consequences that require explanation.

Commitment shapes action of organizational agents through the setting of performance standards. Setting the standard shapes interpretation of the situation, in other words, it forms the metaphor from which the decision maker builds interpretation. Daft and Weick (2001, 253–254) assert that in this way the design of the decision becomes a matter of interpretation before it becomes a matter of deciding. Frames affect what we see and what we ignore, which ultimately determines the scope and content of decision.

Action-based rhetoric in organizations is about setting reference points that the organizational agents need to accomplish. Main set of tools of action based rhetoric is, therefore, assigned in the area of quality management. The foundation of quality management, which can be sufficiently expressed by Deming's (2000) approach, is based on the practice of continuous improvement of the performance through the process of setting higher standards. If the change is to be implemented through the rhetoric of action, the level of performance standards must continuously be increased. Improvement of activities is based on active reflections on what we have done, in other words on learning. Senge et al. (2003, 6) notes that many proponents of organizational change initiatives are not aware of the importance of learning. As a result, the change initiatives are destined not to be realized in their full potential. Without learning, without progress, every system will eventually disband—*non progredi est regredi*—to not go forward is to go backward.

The meaning derived from committing is generally viewed as a process of motivation but it also has an important role in the social construction of reality, which is of great importance to the medium of change—organizational enactment. The process of focusing activity through setting of standards helps in construction of reality by shaping the overall flow of experience through the mechanism of isolating elements that might have impact on the activity that justify commitment to the co-opted purpose.

In the case of the second type of radical decision maker's action-based rhetoric—manipulation—the focus is on the consequences of purposeful action. Since environment is the subject of the construction of the decision maker, the mechanism of manipulation of the environment is a frequent approach to rhetoric in the decision making situation.

The rhetoric of manipulation can be interpreted as a process of involved interpretation. Involvement and commitment to a specific goal ties the decision maker with his behavior. Behavior, in turn, becomes an immutable aspect of one's life and a primary source of interpretations. As Stephen Covey (2004, 46) famously puts it: "Sow a thought, reap an action; sow an action, reap a habit; sow a habit, reap a character; sow a character, reap a destiny."

Explicit behavior, as well as an irrevocable decision, defines the area around which cognitive apparatus must be activated. Once it becomes more difficult to change behavior than belief about the behavior, beliefs are selectively altered in order to justify behavior. This process of striving for internal consistency is an example of cognitive dissonance (Festinger 1962). Elster (1983, 22–25) illustrates the cognitive dissonance through the Aesop's fable "The Fox and the Grapes." In the story, a fox wants to eat some high-hanging grapes but is unable to think of a way to reach them. After some time, the fox reasons that the grapes are probably sour and not worth eating anyway.

Manipulation works because of our need for rationalization. The behavior is rationalized through the process of referring to the characteristics of the environment that support it. The search for meaning of this kind also occurs in a social context where norms and expectations define behavior. Salancik and Pfeffer (1978, 231) call this process a legitimating of behavior—in order to make our behavior more meaningful and in order to be able to explain it to other people, we develop acceptable explanations for each of our actions. The basic idea of manipulation is that people principally try to make sense of the activities to which they feel the strongest obligation. An acceptable explanation for a decision that manipulation provides, as Weick (1995, 167) points out, serves as a seed for further interpretation and action. In other words, in the long run, the form shapes the content.

Process of rhetoric for radical change

As noted in the first chapter, the organizational radical decisions are not the only kind of radical action. The individual radical decisions are more common. The difference is important—in order to make individual radical decision, one does not need rhetoric. I have a friend whose family members never spoke with him after he became a priest. I also know a person whose family never accepted the fact that she changed her sex. Their persuasion did not work, but in both cases they went through with it. This is why driving rhetoric for organizational change is one of leader's most important activities. The job is based on the interpretation of novel perspective to the other members of the organization whose way of thinking about the situation in hand will consequently be altered.

The incremental process of rhetoric for radical change consists of three phases. First, the leader must integrate current situational influences, both external and internal, to the initial mental representation. This is done through initial presentation and negotiation of the radical mental model with several people of the leader's confidence, usually, the top management team. In the first phase, the initial mental representation changes through the process of harmonization—it develops, becomes more specific, refined or reduced by the constructs of others. The second phase is based on the alignment of the radical representation with key stakeholders. This phase constitutes the frame in which rhetoric of action takes place. Dissemination of radical representations to other members of the organization through the activities is the third phase of the process. From this perspective, the role of a leader is to encourage people to go ahead with certain activities and simultaneously to seek out new signs that will direct further action.

Changing minds is an incremental kind of process—some buy-in to the new viewpoint at the beginning and some never. Also, the rhetoric process of implementation of radical change, as pointed out in previous segments of the chapter, is based either on the process driven by beliefs or action. In respect to the described process of rhetoric for implementation of radical change in complex organization, belief-driven rhetoric is main approach of the second phase while action-driven rhetoric is principal mode of the third phase of the implementation model.

As already stated, the initial mental representation changes through the phase of harmonization—it develops, becomes more specific, refined or fragmented by the constructs of other members of the organization.

Any organizational change, particularly radical one, rarely occurs suddenly. Habitually, it is a matter of building consensus through socially constructed negotiation (Berger and Luckmann 1966). Through the process of consensus building, centers of power are trying to position themselves on what they consider to be a better position in the new design. The principal activity of the "old aristocracy" is to discourage implementation of the radical changes in organizational enactment. Understanding the different views on the situation of decision making is a key prerequisite for success of the implementation of radical decisions.

After a longer or shorter time of negotiation with the key stakeholders, the next phase of radical decision implementation is action-based rhetoric which comprises the rest of the organization. Sensegiving driven by action is the crucial part of the implementation of radical decisions. From this perspective, the role of a leader is to encourage the people to perform designated activities and look for new signs that will direct further action. The sensemaking process initiated by the radical decision maker has the iterative character. It is based on the understanding of the situation in which the decision maker is as well as on trying to gain a little bit better comprehension of where she wants to be. Plans that arise from the strategic direction of the organization provide the purpose and a vision of what the organization wants to achieve.

The incremental nature of the radical decision is reflected in the second and third step of the process of radical decision implementation—the sensegiving phases. A key process for successful implementation of radical change is the creation of derived interpretations of the situation. Transposition of the new meaning of the situation, compressed in the loadstar, cannot be conveyed to the entire organization at once. Each interpretation is formed separately, and some people need more time and incentives that the others. As people are crystallizing their understanding of the situation, through the resulting action they make the initial representation more concrete and more tuned.

In the process described earlier a lot of resources are consumed in "preparing the ground"—in activities such as building of coalitions and establishment of sensemaking reference points through planning and so on. The rhetoric approach of this kind, which we can call the managerial approach to radical decision making, is necessary for the implementation of the radical decision in most of the complex organizations. However, the leader can avoid the second phase of the process and immediately move on to the rhetoric of activities. This model of rhetoric of radical change can be referred to as an entrepreneurial approach. In the case of the entrepreneurial approach time is not lost on negotiation about the reference points for sensemaking because in this case the leader's charismatic aura performs part of the rhetorical job.

Radical rhetoric as *parrhesia*

After the insight in the process of implementation of radical change through "conventional" means of arguing, expectation setting, committing and manipulation, the last segment of the chapter describes the *parrhesian* approach to radical rhetoric. It is a specific rhetoric method which is, in my opinion, the most suitable for radical persuasion. Coming from the perspective that leading radical change is about setting the path and getting things done, which demands a radical paradigm shift, a change of mind and eventually a change of heart, I argue that the radical leader's most important peculiarity should be truthfulness.

It is common knowledge that nobody tells the truth these days. In the post-modern, "anything goes, and nothing means anything" world, the concept of truth seems obsolete. Mainstream approach in human relations, driven by the mass media position, is overwhelmed by the so-called political correctness—do not run afoul of anybody, endure everything, do not say the truth to anyone's face. We are derived to instrumental minds that keep us from exiting the Platonic cave into the light. Exiting one's own immaturity—using our own mind without anyone's tutoring and custody. Habermas (1981) has spoken of the "unfinished project of modernity," not without irony. Overwhelming feeling of lostness is defining characteristic of today's mindset. Men do not know what to believe or what to do.

Truth however exists, and it is useful. Radical decision maker knows it. He is not a post-modernist. Leading radical change is about setting the path, and finally settling in the right place, about getting things done. Radical change calls for a paradigm shift. A change of mind. A change of perspective. A change of heart. As I said before in the discussion about radical leader's identity, in order to implement radical change in complex organizational settings the leader does not have to be a superman, not even "a hero type," but I do argue that he has to have one specific characteristic, rather scarce these days—he has to be truthful.

The act of telling the truth without either embellishment or concealment is known as the *parrhesia*. Parrh´esia has most frequently been translated as "free speech" or "freedom of speech," but recently a number of scholars express greater satisfaction with the term "frank speech" (Foucault 2001; Monoson 2000; Henderson 1998; Momigliano 1973). In short *parrhesia* may be interpreted as an open, free and daring speech.

Michael Foucault (2010) revived the term *parrhesia* in explaining the idea of "true life" in Greek philosophy typical for the Cynic philosophers. He deals with the subject in his two final lecture courses at the College de France—"The Government of Self" (2011) and "The Courage of Truth" (20). The chief object of concern is the *parrhesia* as a practice of self that is centered on the relation of the subject to truth, and how through engaging in *parrhesia* one freely constitutes one's subjectivity. Foucault very clearly connects *parrhesia* to the Kantian tradition of critical philosophy. It is in Socrates, Foucault says, that the care of the self first manifests itself as the parrhesia. Also, according to Plato, Socrates possesses the character traits of responsibility for one's own speech (*parr´esia*), goodwill (*eunoia*) and a commitment to knowledge (*epist´em´e*) (McCoy 2007, 5). Besides Foucault, Kant and Socrates, the issue of pursuing the truth is also present at the other side of the philosophical spectrum. For instance, St. Thomas Aquinas speaks of the three Transcendental—the True, the Good and the Beautiful.

Why is truth important in implementing radical change? Why can radical decision not be sophist manipulation of others?

The initial thought is just the opposite—illusion is what counts, what people think of us, not what is true. If 80 percent of the neurological stimulus comes from sense of sight, and if most cognitive processes are based on the ways to simplify reasoning, we can conclude that the superficiality is very important—the style is more important than the substance. In many cases that are so, but not in the case of implementation of radical decisions.

There are four key reasons why the radical decision maker must not be resourceful and a permanent reckoner of the truth. Why the leader cannot always recite the different truth, according to the need of listeners, in order to be liked and to meet their interests? Before I bring forth the four reasons one additional note needs to be made. Guardini (1995, 106) puts it well in his assertion that truth is the power, but only if we do not require the immediate effectiveness, but if we cultivate patience and count on the long run. The truth is, therefore, realized in time. If we do not have the patience for the truth to mature, we will have to bear consequences. It is the very reason why the "Wall Street" system of management efficiency, based on the short-term objectives, built on the imperative for capital appreciation on quarterly basis, will keep collapsing until its inevitable stumble.

The first reason for the importance of truth in the implementation of radical changes is that although lies might bring short-term results, in the long run, the liar always ends up unmasked. That way the manipulator loses the illusion of character and as such he cannot change people's minds. The problem of lies, as Frankfurt (2006, 36–37) puts it, is that a liar loses the confidence of all people who witnesses the act, not just the directly affected person. Lying in the long run leads to decay and ruin. Another reason for the importance of truth in implementation of change is that the truth is simple, while lies burden and consume the cognitive capacity of the decision maker. The saying "truth will set you free" proves the point perfectly. The same text also describes the third reason truth is of crucial importance for the implementation of radical decisions—lie closes in itself, narrows horizons of the decision makers and prevents finding different solutions. Dishonesty puts us in the frame of causality that, due to the possibility of creating illogical relations, avoids any significant change. A falsehood is centripetal while the truth is centrifugal: it breaks out. The fourth reason is that a lie leads to fear. Patience, which is a prerequisite for using the power of truth, is a sign of selflessness. It is one of the reasons why we say that humility is a key feature of the identity of the radical leaders. We are patient if we do not seek instantaneous reaction from the others because we have no expectation that they will immediately meet our goals. But if we do have such expectations, and they are not met, we will get discouraged and the contrary process will be initiated.

Now we can see that *parrhesia* in principle is not another kind of rhetoric, as argumentation, expectation setting, committing and manipulation are. The intention of rhetoric is not telling the truth, but being persuasive. This is why the rhetoric uses various techniques to achieve this intention. Rhetoric discourse is always ornamental and theatrical, and rhetorician does not care for his attitude toward the truth. The rhetorician's intention is that the listener needs to forget themselves, to be fascinated by rhetorical approach rather that with the truth.

Except the importance of truth in organizational discourse, two other aspects of *parrhesia* are important in implementing radical change. First, *parrhesia* is an important part of unfolding the concept of mesmerizing attraction framed in the term "charisma." Charisma can be defined as the ability to capture the attention and communicate in a vivid and clear manner. Second, the *parrhesian* style provides determination, which is also a very important leadership trait. When a person speaks as if something is true or important, then others are more likely to believe them. A radical leader speaks with authority because she understands the philosophical background that derived the logical results of his actions. In contrast, if we are tentative and use vague language, then others are less likely to believe us.

The leader who uses *parrhesian* rhetorical style takes individual and social elements of argumentations in a specific way. She is entirely engaged in the dialogue. Discourse and meaning of the speaker is inseparable. If listener is against the speech, he is against the narrator. Such a rhetorician is focused on one thing—reaction of the listener, change in his attitude.

The key of radical rhetoric is to change people's minds. There are two ways the radical rhetoric of *parrhesia* can help us do it—argumentation and setting an example.

A leader of radical change has to be a master of argumentation rhetoric, a master of principled persuasion that takes place in a dialogue. The focal point of a leader's one-to-one conversations with other organizational agents is the persons themselves. It means that when the radical leader talks with an organizational agent, he does not do so with ulterior motives: he speaks to the person for their own good not just for the good of the "cause" or out of some selfish reason. In making radical change happen we do not want that people just to do something, we want them to be on our side, to change their minds. Therefore, the radical leader attracts and repels people not because he would win arguments, but because he illuminates their hearts. It is a dialog for truth that echoes in the heart until it eventually changes thinking and action. Where a better book would start a discussion—on the topic of the dialog, my book will end. As for this attempt, it is enough to call attention to the fact that the *parrhesian* approach to radical rhetoric focuses more on the heart than on the intellect. It holds that our decisions are often beyond the merely rational or reasonable.

Besides the dialog, the *parrhesian* influence on radical rhetoric has another face—the *parrhesia* is not only about telling the truth but also about living it. There is a huge difference between knowledge and experience. Knowledge alone is not enough. Knowledge will never decisively and permanently change anyone, but the experience will, if it is lasting and if it goes deep into one's mind.

For the radical decision maker, therefore, important is not only the theoretical truth-telling, but also the *forma vitae*, practical, physical truth-telling in public, in front of people and for the people. Such an approach requires specific stylistics of existence—rhetoric of example that instills beliefs without argumentation. Gandhi was in the first lines of the protests and Mother Theresa tended dying lepers day after day for decades. Also, the core of the Socratic *parrhesia* is positioned in his focus on the accord between the way one lives (bios) and the rational discourse or account (logos). One might or might not think in a way what would justify how one lives. In fact, Socrates boldly speaks the truth; he is not afraid of the tyrant who wants to stop him. Unlike the sophist or the rhetorician who speaks nicely, but is not "worthy" of his speech, because he do not think and live what he says, Socrates stood by his words.

In the implementation of radical decisions, the leader challenges assumptions and thinking. In order to elicit the expected response from the listeners he often uses rhetorical questions and the Socratic method. He often speaks in riddles, parables, and imponderables that re-arrange the human mind.

Special means of *parrhesia*, available to the radical decision maker is irony. Already in Aristotle (2010, 1124b), the irony is defined as an expression of *parrhesia*. The irony is desirable if its goal is not to make fun of somebody but if it intends to open the listener to the truth, to stimulate the mind. Irony is indirect speech: something is confirmed, and actually it is negatively stated; we agree with something, and actually the disagreement and contradiction comes to the fore. Irony wants to "poke" the other, wake him from his dormancy for the truth. What is great and glorious, in fact, calls for irony because it demands to be indirectly communicated in order to attract the attention of the other.

Parrhesian rhetoric leads to avoiding large differences in interpretations. In other words, to be able to make effective decisions, leaders must find a way of focusing on the process of interpretation. Otherwise, members of the organization will be overwhelmed and preoccupied with different interpretations of their past activities. The best way to realign the interpretations is to hold on to the truth. *Parrhesian* argumentation, way of enforcing the truth, is the most important approach that leaders have available to reinforce the acceptance of their own beliefs, values and assumptions. As the organization develops, the leader's postulations become shared and part of the culture of the organization. New members now experience these cultural assumptions as a given, no longer as something to be discussed.

Since the change in listener's sensemaking process is the center of radical decisions, the *parrhesian* rhetoric must be compelling enough to engage the entire person. The leader who wants to implement radical change has to hone his rhetorical skills to perfection, but not solely in the service of debate or some discrete set of doctrines cut-off from real life and imposed upon other persons without discretion. The leader's rhetoric has to embrace the whole of life—the entirety of man's existence. Making a difference between personal life and work does not work when it comes to committing to radical change. It is the same mind at the office and at home. Radical change is about reinterpreting, resetting, reforming, renewing, restoring, refocusing, reevaluating, reprioritization and reinventing. Radical rhetoric needs to transform our thinking; and to some extent even our ideologies, our worldviews and our way of life.

Bibliography

Ackermann, Fran, and Colin Eden. 2011. *Making Strategy: Mapping Out Strategic Success*. Thousand Oaks: Sage Publications.

Adams, Frederick, and Kenneth Aizawa. 2010. *The Bounds of Cognition*. Oxford: Wiley-Backwell.

Aquinas, Thomas. 2006. "Summa Theologica, Part II-II (Secunda Secundae)." In: The Project Gutenberg. http://www.gutenberg.org/cache/epub/18755/pg18755.html.

Argyris, Chris. 1976. "Theories of Action That Inhibit Individual Learning." *American Psychologist* 31 (9):638–654.

———. 1982. "The Executive Mind and Double-Loop Learning." *Organizational Dynamics* 11 (2):5–22.

Aristotle. 1868. "Eudemian Ethics." In. London: Heinemann. https://archive.org/details/athenianconstituooarisuoft.

———. 1893. "The Nicomachean Ethics." In. London: Kegan Paul, Trench, Truebner & Co. http://oll.libertyfund.org/titles/903.

———. 2009. "Metaphysics." In: The Internet Classics Archive. http://classics.mit.edu/Aristotle/metaphysics.html.

———. 2010. *Rhetoric*: ReadaClassic.com.

Arygris, Chris, and A Donald Schön. 1978. *Organizational Learning: A Theory of Action Perspective*, Addison-Wesley Series on Organization Development. Reading: Addison-Wesley.

Ball, Terence. 2012. *Lincoln: Political Writings and Speeches*. Cambridge: Cambridge University Press.

Baracskai, Zoltán, Viktor Dörfler and Jolán Velencei. 2005. *Majstor i kalfa*. Zagreb: Sinergija.

Barnard, Chester I. 1938. *The Functions of the Executive*. Cambridge, MA: Harvard University Press.

Barr, Pamela S., J. L. Stimpert and Anne S. Huff. 1992. "Cognitive Change, Strategic Action, and Organizational Renewal." *Strategic Management Journal* 13:15–36.

Bartlett, Frederic. 2010. "Remembering—A Study in Experimental and Social Psychology." In. Cambridge: Cambridge University Press. http://dx.doi.org/10.1017/CBO9780511759185.

Basler, Roy P. 1989. *Abraham Lincoln: Speeches and Writings 1832–1858*. Library of America.

Basler, Roy P., and Carl Sandburg. 2008. *Abraham Lincoln: His Speeches and Writings*. Da Capo Press.

Beck, Nikolaus, Josef Brüderl and Michael Woywode. 2008. "Momemtum or Declaration? Theoretical and Methodological Reflections on the Analysis of Organizational Change." *Academy of Management Journal*. 51 (3):413–435.

Beck, Ulrich. 1992. *Risk Society: Towards a New Modernity*. Thousand Oaks: Sage Publications.

Berger, Peter L., and Thomas Luckmann. 1966. *The Social Construction of Reality: A Treatise in the Sociology of Knowledge*. Garden City: Anchor Books.

Bible. 1989. "The King James Bible." In: The Project Gutenberg. http://www.gutenberg.org/files/10/10-h/10-h.htm.

Billig, Michael. 1989. *Arguing and Thinking: A Rhetorical Approach to Social Psychology*. Cambridge: Cambridge University Press.

Boulding, Kenneth E. 1956. "General System Theory: The Skeleton of Science." *Management Science* 2:197–208.

———. 1978. *Ecodynamics: A New Theory of Societal Evolution*. Thousand Oaks: Sage Publications.

Brehmer, Berndt. 1990. "Strategies in Real-Time Dynamic Decision-Making." In *Insights in Decision-making: A Tribute to Hillel J. Einhorn*, edited by R. Hogarth. Chicago: University of Chicago Press, 262–279.

Broadbent, Donald. 1958. *Perception and Communication*. London: Pergamon Press.

Brown, Andrew D. 2000. "Making Sense of Inquiry Sensemaking." *Journal of Management Studies* 37 (1):45–75.

Brown, Roger. 1958. *Words and Things.* New York: The Free Press.

Bruner, Jerome. 1986. *Actual Minds, Possible Worlds.* Cambridge, MA: Harvard University Press.

———. 1990. *Acts of Meaning.* Cambridge: Harvard University Press.

Brunsson, Nils. 1982. "The Irrationality of Action and Action Rationality: Decisions, Ideologies and Organizational Actions." *Journal of Management Studies* 19:29–44.

Caesar, Julius. 2007a. *The Civil War.* Translated by Jane F. Gardner. London: Penguin.

———. 2007b. *The Conquest of Gaul.* Translated by Jane F. Gardner. London: Penguin.

Carson, Shelley. 2010. *Your Creative Brain: Seven Steps to Maximize Imagination, Productivity, and Innovation in Your Life.* Hoboken, NY: Wiley.

Cassirer, Ernst. 1946. *The Myth of the State.* New Heaven: Yale University Press.

Chesterton, G. K. 1908. "Orthodoxy." In: The Project Gutenberg. http://www.gutenberg.org/cache/epub/130/pg130.html.

Chia, Robert. 1999. "A 'Rhizomic' Model of Organizational Change and Transformation: Perspective from a Metaphysics of Change." *British Journal of Management* 10 (3):209–277.

Ching, Tao Te. 2012. "A Book about the Way and Power of the Way." In. Boston: manybooks.net. http://manybooks.net/titles/laotzuetext95taote10.html.

Cohen, Michael D., James G. March and Johan P. Olsen. 1972. "A Garbage Can Model of Organizational Choice." *Administrative Science Quarterly* 17:25.

Cornelissen, Joep P. 2004. "What Are We Playing At? Theatre, Organization, and the Use of Metaphor." *Organization Studies* 25 (5):705–726.

———. 2006. "Metaphor and the Dynamics of Knowledge in Organization Theory: A Case Study of the Organizational Identity Metaphor*." *Journal of Management Studies* 43 (4):683–709.

Cornelissen, Joep P., Cliff Oswick, Lars Thøger Christensen and Nelson Phillips. 2008. "Metaphor in Organizational Research: Context, Modalities and Implications for Research—Introduction." *Organization Studies* 29 (1):7–22.

Coulson, Seana. 2001. *Semantic Leaps: Frame-Shifting and Conceptual Blending in Meaning Construction*. Cambridge: Cambridge University Press.

Covey, Stephen R. 2004. *The 7 Habits of Highly Effective People: Powerful Lessons in Personal Change*: Free Press.

Cyert, Richard M., and James G. March. 1963. *A Behavioral Theory of the Firm*. Englewod Cliffs, NJ: Prentice Hall.

Czarniawska, Barbara. 1997. *Narrating the Organization: Dramas of Institutional Identity*. University of Chicago Press.

———. 1998. *A Narrative Approach to Organization Studies*. SAGE Publications.

Daft, Richard L., and Norman B. MacIntosh. 1981. "A Tentative Exploration into the Amount and Equivocality of Information Processing in Organizational Work Units." *Administrative Science Quarterly* 26 (2):207–224.

Daft, Richard L., and Karl E. Weick. 1984. "Toward a Model of Organizations as Interpretation System." *Academy of Management Review* 9:284–295.

———. 2001. "Toward a Model of Organizations as Interpretation Systems." In *Making Sense of the Organization*, edited by E. Weick, Karl, 241–259. Malden: Blackwell Publishing.

Damásio, Anthony. 2005. *Descartes' Error: Emotion, Reason, and the Human Brain*. London: Penguin Books.

Davenport, Thomas H., and John C. Beck. 2002. *Attention Economy: Understanding the New Currency of Business*. Cambridge, MA: Harvard Business School.

De Geus, Arie. 1997. *The Living Company*. Cambridge: Harvard University Press.

de Saint Exupery, Antoine. 1943. *The Little Prince*. Translated by K. Woods. New York: Reynal and Hitchcock.

Deming, W. Edwards. 2000. *The New Economics: For Industry, Government, Education*. Cambridge: MIT Press.

Denning, Stephen. 2004. "Telling Tales." *Harvard Business Review* 82 (5):122–129.

———. 2007. *The Secret Language of Leadership—How Leaders Inspire Action through Narrative*. San Francisco: Jossey-Bass.

Descartes, Rene. 1984. *Principles of Philosophy*. Translated by V. R. Miller and R. P. Miller. New York: Springer Netherlands.

Dörfler, Viktor, Zoltán Baracskai and Jolán Velencei. 2009. "Knowledge Levels: 3-D Model of the Levels of Expertise." AoM 2009: Annual Conference of the Academy of Management, Chicago, IL.

Dyer, Jeff, Hall B. Gregersen and Clayton M. Christensen. 2011. *The Innovator's DNA: Mastering the Five Skills of Disruptive Innovators*. Cambridge, MA: Harvard Business Press.

Eden, Colin, Sue Jones and David Sims. 1979. *Thinking in Organizations*. London: The MacMillan Press.

Eden, Colin, and J. C. Spender, eds. 1998. *Managerial and Organizational Cognition: Theory, Methods and Research*. Thousand Oaks: Sage Publications.

Elster, Jon. 1983. *Sour Grapes: Studies in the Subversion of Rationality*. Cambridge University Press.

Emerson, Richard 1962. "Power-Dependence Relations." *American Sociological Review* 27:31–41.

Erez, Miriam, and Christopher P. Earley. 1993. *Culture, Self-identitiy, and Work*. New York: Oxford University Press.

Ericson, Thomas. 2001. "Sensemaking in Organisations—Towards a Conceptual Framework for Understanding Strategic Change." *Scandinavian Journal of Management* 17 (1):109–131.

Eysenck, Micahel, and Mark T. Keane. 2002. "Attention and Performace Limitations." In *Foundations of Cognitive Psychology*, edited by Daniel J. Levitin, 363–399. Cambridge: MIT Press.

Eysenck, Michael W. 2001. *Principles of Cognitive Psychology*. Edited by Michael W. Eysenck, Simon Green and Nicky Hayes. 2nd ed, *Principles of Psychology*. Sussex: Psychology Press.

Festinger, Leon. 1962. *A Theory of Cognitive Dissonance*: Stanford University Press.

Fiske, Suzan T., and Shelley E. Taylor. 1991. *Social Cognition*. Reading: Addison-Wesley.

Follett, Mary Parker. 1924. *Creative Experience*. New York: Longmans Green.

Foucault, Michael. 2001. *Fearless Speech*. Semiotext(e).

———. 2010. *The Government of Selves and Others—Lectures at the College de France 1982–1983*. Translated by Graham Burchell. New York: Palgrave MacMillan.

———. 2011. *The Courage of Truth*. New York: Palgrave Macmillan.

Frankfurt, Harry G. 2006. *On Truth*. Knopf.

Freud, Sigmund. 1911. "The Interpretation of Dreams." In: Psych Web. http://www.psywww.com/books/interp/toc.htm.

Gergen, Kenneth J. 1982. *Toward Transformation in Social Knowledge*. New York: Springer-Verlag.

Giddens, Antony. 1976. *New Rules of Sociological Method*. London: Hutchinson.

Gigerenzer, Gerd. 2007. *Snaga intuicije: inteligencija nesvjesnog*. Zagreb: Algoritam.

Gioia, Dennis A. 1986. "Symbols, Scripts, and Sensemaking: Creating Meaning in the Organizational Experience." In *The Thinking Organization*, edited by H. Sims and D. A. Gioia, 49–74. San Francisco: Jossey-Bass.

Gioia, Dennis A., and Kumar Chittipeddi. 1991. "Sensemaking and Sensegiving in Strategic Change Initiation." *Strategic Management Journal* 12:433–448.

Giorello, Giulio, and Corrado Sinigaglia. 2007. "Perception in Action." *Acta BIOMED* 78 (1):49–57.

Gladwell, Malcolm. 2008. *Outliers: The Story of Success*. New York: Allen Lane.

Gobet, Fernand, and Herbert Alexander Simon. 1996a. "Recall of Random and Distorted Chess Positions: Implications for the Theory of Expertise." *Memory & Cognition* 24 (4):493–503.

———. 1996b. "Templates in Chess Memory: Mechanism for Re-calling Several Boards." *Cognitive Psychology* 31 (1):1–40.

———. 2000. "Five Seconds or Sixty? Presentation Time in Expert Memory." *Cognitive Science* 24 (4):651–682.

Goldstein, Bruce E. 2010. *Sensation and Perception*. Belmont, CA: Wadsworth.

Gravlee, Scott G. 2000. "Aristotle on Hope." *Journal of History of Philosophy* 28 (4):461–477.

Guardini, Romano. 1995. *Stationen und Ruckblicke—Berichte uber mein Leben*. Mainz: Paderborn.

Guenther, Kim. 2002. "Memory." In *Foundations of Cognitive Psychology*, edited by Daniel J. Levitin, 311–361. Cambridge: MIT Press.

Habermas, Jurgen, and Seyla Ben-Habib. 1981. "Modernitiy versus Postmodernity." *New German Critique* 22 (Special Issue on Modernism):3–14.

Henderson, Jeffrey. 1998. "Attic Old Comedy, Frank Speech, and Democracy." In *Democracy, Empire, and the Arts in Fifth-Century*

Athens, edited by Deborah Boedeker and Kurt A. Raaflaub, 255–273. Cambridge, MA: Harvard University Press.

Hill, Robert C., and Michael Levenhagen. 1995. "Metaphors and Mental Models: Sensemaking and Sensegiving in Innovative and Entrepreneurial Activities." *Journal of Management* 21 (6):1057–1074.

Hodgkinson, Gerard, and Paul R. Sparrow. 2002. *The Competent Organization*. Buckingham: Open University Press.

Hume, David. 1974. "An Enquiry Concerning Human Understanding; Dialoges Concerning Natural Religion." In *The Empiricists*, edited by J. Lock, G. Berkeley and D. Hume. Doubleday: Anchor Books, 307–431.

James, William. 2007. *The Principles of Psychology*. Vol. 1. New York: Cosimo Classics.

———. 2007. *The Principles of Psychology*. Vol. 2. New York: Cosimo Classics.

Johnson-Laird, Phillip N. 1983. *Mental Models: Towards a Cognitive Science of Language, Inference and Consciousness*. Cambridge: Harvard University Press.

———. 2010. "Mental Models and Human Reasoning." *Proceedings of the National Academy of Sciences*.

Jung, Carl G. 1983. *The Psychology of the Transference*. Routledge.

Kahneman, Daniel. 1973. *Attention and Effort*. New Jersey: Prentice-Hall.

———. 2013. *Thinking, Fast and Slow*. New York: Farrar, Straus and Giroux.

Kahneman, Daniel, and Amos Tversky. 1972. "Subjective Pobability: A Judgment of Representativeness." *Cognitive Psychology* 3:430–454.

———. 1979. "Prospect Theory: An Analysis of Decision under Risk." *Econometrica* 47 (2):263–291.

Kelly, George. 1955. *The Psychology of Personal Constructs*. Vol. I and II. New York: Norton.

Klein, Gary. 2008. "Naturalistic Decision Making." *Human Factors: The Journal of the Human Factors and Ergonomics Society* 50:456–460.

Kuhn, Thomas S. 2002. *Struktura znanstvenih revolucija*. Zagreb: Jesenski i Turk.

Lachman, Roy, Janet L. Lachman and Earl C. Butterfield. 1979. *Cognitive Psychology and Information Processing: An Introduction*. Hillsdale, NJ: Lawrence Erlbaum Associates, Publishers.

Lear, Jonathan. 2006. *Radical Hope: Ethics in the Face of Cultural Devastation*. Harvard University Press.

Levy, Steven. 1992. *Artificial Life: A Report from the Frontier Where Computers Meet Biology*. Vintage Books.

Lewin, Kurt. 1951. *Field Theory in Social Science: Selected Theoretical Papers*. Harper.

Lipshitz, Raanan. 1989. "'Either a Medal or a Corporal': The Effects of Success and Failure on the Evaluation of Decision Making and Decision Makers." *Organizational Behavior and Human Decision Processes* 44 (3):380–395.

Locke, John. 2004. "An Essay Concerning Humane Understanding, Volume I." In: The Project Gutenberg. http://www.gutenberg.org/cache/epub/10615/pg10615.html.

Louis, Meryl R. 1980. "Surprise and Sensemaking: What Newcomers Experience in Entering Unfamiliar Organizational Settings." *Administrative Science Quarterly* 25.

Mabillard, Amanda. 2000. "What Inspired Shakespeare?" Shakespeare Online. http://www.shakespeare-online.com/faq/shakespeareinspired.html.

March, G., James. 1994. *A Primer on Decision Making: How Decisions Happen*. New York: The Free Press.

March, James G., and Johan P. Olsen. 1976. *Ambiguity and Choice in Organizations*. Bergen, Norway: Universitetsforlaget.

March, James G., and Herbert Alexander Simon. 1993. *Organizations*. 2nd ed. Oxford: Blackwell.

Mason, Richard O., and Ian Mitroff. 1981. *Challenging Strategic Planning Assumptions, Theory, Cases, and Techniques*. New York: John Wiley.

McCarthy, George E. 2001. *Objectivity and the Silence of Reason: Weber, Habermas, and the Methodological Disputes in German Sociology*. Transaction Publishers.

McCloskey, Deirdre. 2006. *The Bourgeois Vitues—Ethics for an Age of Commerce*. Chicago: University of Chicago Press.

McCoy, Marina. 2007. *Plato on the Rhetoric of Philosophers and Sophists*. Cambridge: Cambridge University Press.

Mead, George Herbert. 1934. *Mind, Self and Society*. Chicago: University of Chicago Press.

———. 1956. *The Social Psychology of George Herbert Mead*. Edited by A. M. Strauss. Chicago: University of Chicago Press.

Mead, George Herbert, Charles W. Morris, John M. Brewster, Albert M. Dunham and David L. Miller. 1938. *The Philosophy of the Act*. Chicago: University of Chicago Press.

Mervis, Carolyn, and Eleanor Rosch. 1981. "Categorization of Natrual Objects." *Annual Review of Psychology* 32:89–115.

Mintzberg, Henry. 1973. "Strategy-Making in Three Modes." *California Management Review* 16 (2):44–53.

Mintzberg, Henry, Bruce Ahlstrand and Joseph Lampel. 1998. *Strategy Safari: The Complete Guide through the Wilds of Strategic Management.* 2nd ed. London: FT Prentice Hall.

Monoson, Sara S. 2000. *Plato's Democratic Entanglements: Athenian Politics and the Practice of Philosophy.* Princeton: Princeton University Press.

Morgan, Gareth. 1980. "Paradigms, Metaphors, and Puzzle Solving in Organization Theory." *Administrative Science Quarterly* 25:605–622.

———. 2006. *Images of Organization.* Thousand Oaks: Sage Publications.

Morgan, Gareth, Peter J. Frost and Louis R. Pondy. 1983. "Organizational Symbolism." In *Organizational Symbolism*, edited by L. R Pondy, P. J. Frost, G. Morgan and T. C. Dandridge, 24. Greenwich: CT: JAI.

Neisser, Ulric. 1976. *Cognition and Reality: Principles and Implications of Cognitive Psychology.* W. H. Freeman and Co.

Newton, Issac. 2004. Untitled treatise on Revelation.

Nonaka, Ikujiro, and Teruo Yamanouchi. 1989. "Managing Innovation as a Self-Renewing Process." *Journal of Business Venturing* 4.299–315.

O'Neill, John J. 1996. *Prodigal Genius: The Life of Nikola Tesla.* New Mexico: Brotherhood of Life.

Palmer, Ian, and Richard Dunford. 1996. "Conflicting Uses of Metaphors: Reconceptualizing Their Use in the Field of Organizational Change." *The Academy of Management Review* 21 (3):691–717.

Pettigrew, Andrew M., and Evelyn M. Fenton. 2000. "Complexities and Dualities in Innovative Forms of Organizing." In *The Innovating Organization*, edited by A. M. Pettigrew and E. M. Fenton. London: Sage, 279–301.

Pfeffer, Jeffrey. 1981. "Management as Symbolic Action." In *Research in Organizational Behavior* edited by L. L. Cummings and B. M. Staw, 1–51. Greenwich: CT: JAI.

Plato. 2008. "The Republic." In: The Project Gutenberg. http://www.gutenberg.org/files/1497/1497-h/1497-h.htm.

Polanyi, Michael. 1957. "Problem Solving." *The British Journal for the Philosophy of Science* 8 (30):89–103.

———. 1964. *Personal Knowledge: Towards a Post-Critical Philosophy*. New York Harper Torchbooks.

Porac, Joseph F., Howard Thomas and Charles Baden-Fuller. 1989. "Competitve Groups as Cognitive Communities: The Case of Scottish Knitwear Manufacturers." *Journal of Management Studies* 26:39–416.

Prietula, Michael J., and Herbert Alexander Simon. 1989. "The Experts in Your Midst." *Harvard Business Review* 67 (January–February):120–124.

Putnam, Linda L., and Suzanne Boys. 2006. "Revisiting Metaphors of Organizational Communication The SAGE Handbook of Organization Studies." In *The SAGE Handbook of Organization Studies*, edited by S. Clegg, C. Hardy, T. Lawrence and W. Nord, 541–577. London: Sage Publications.

Ratzinger, Joseph. 2012. *Djetinjstvo Isusovo*. Split: Verbum.

Root-Bernstein, Robert S., and Michele Root-Bernstein. 1999. *Sparks of Genius: The Thirteen Thinking Tools of the World's Most Creative People*. Houghton Mifflin Company.

Ross, Michael. 1989. "Relation of Implicit Theories to the Construction of Personal Histories." *Psychological Review* 96:341–357.

Rumelhart, David E., and Donald A. Norman. 1988. "Representation in Memory." In *Stevens' Handbook of Experimental Psychology*, edited by Richard C. Atkinson, Richard J. Herrnstein, Gardner Lindzey and R. Duncan Luce, 511–587. New York: John Wiley & Sons.

Salancik, Gerald R. 1977. "Commitment and the Control of Organizational Behavior and Belief." In *New Directions in Organizational Behaviour*, edited by Barry M. Staw and Gerald R. Salancik, 1–54. Chicago: St. Clair.

Salancik, Gerald Robert, and Margaret Cooper Brindle. 1997. "The Social Ideologies of Power in Organizational Decisions." In *Organizational Decision Making*, edited by Zur Shapira. Cambridge: Cambridge University Press.

Salancik, Gerald R., and Jeffrey Pfeffer. 1978. "A Social Information Processing Approach to Job Attitudes and Task Design." *Administrative Science Quarterly* 23:224–253.

Schacter, Daniel L. 1996. *Searching for Memory: The Brain, the Mind, and the Past*. New York: Basic Books.

Schön, A. Donald. 1963. *Displacement of Concepts*. London: Tavistock.

———. 1991. *The Reflective Practitioner: How Professionals Think in Action*. Aldershot: Ashgate Publishing Limited. Original edition, 1983.

Schumpeter, Joseph A. 1934. *The Theory of Economic Development.* Cambridge: Harvard University Press.

Schwartzman, Helen B. 1989. *The Meeting: Gatherings in Organizations and Communities.* New York: Plenum.

Senge, Peter, Art Kleiner, Charlotte Roberts, Richard Ross, George Roth and Bryan Smith. 2003. *Ples promjene.* Zagreb: Mozaik knjiga.

Senge, Peter M. 1990. *The Fifth Discipline: The Art and Practice of the Learning Organization.* New York, NY: Doubleday Currency.

Simon, Herbert A., and Craig A. Kaplan. 1989. "Foundations of Cognitive Science." In *The Foundations of Cognitive Science*, edited by M. I. Posner, 1–48. Cambridge: MA: MIT Press.

Simon, Herbert Alexander. 1977. *The New Science of Management Decision.* 3rd ed. New Jersey: Prentice-Hall.

———. 1987. "Making Management Decisions: The Role of Intuition and Emotion." *Academy of Management Executive* 1 (1):57–64.

———. 1997. *Administrative Behavior: A Study of Decision-Making Processes in Administrative Organization.* 4th ed. New York: The Free Press.

Smircich, Linda, and Gareth Morgan. 1982. "Leadership: The Management of Meaning." *Journal of Applied Behavioral Science* 18:257–273.

Smircich, Linda, and Charles Stubbard. 1985. "Strategic Management in an Enacted World." *Academy of Management Review* 10:724–736.

Snyder, Mark. 1984. "When Belief Creates Reality." *Advances in experimental social psychology* 18:247–305.

Spender, J. C. 1998. "The Dynamics of Individual and Organizational Knowledge." In *Managerial and Organizational Cognition: Theory, Methods and Research*, edited by Colin Eden and J. C. Spender. Thousand Oaks: Sage Publications, 13–37.

Spender, J. C., and Colin Eden. 1998. "Introduction." In *Managerial and Organizational Cognition: Theory, Methods and Research*, edited by Colin Eden and J. C. Spender, 1–13. Thousand Oaks: Sage Publications.

Starbuck, William H. 1976. "Organizatons and Their Environments." In *Handbook of Industrial and Organizational Behavior*, edited by M. D. Dunnette, 1081. Chicago: Rand McNally.

Starbuck, William H., and Frances J. Milliken. 1988. "Executives' Perceptual Filters: What They Notice and How They Make Sense." In

The Executive Effect: Concepts and Methods for Studying Top Managers, edited by D. C. Hambrick, 35–65. Greenwich: CT: JAI.

Stravinsky, Igor. 1970. *Poetics of Music in the Form of Six Lessons*. Cambridge: Harvard University Press.

Suetonius, Tranquillus C. 2006. "The Lives Of The Twelve Caesars." In: The Project Gutenberg. http://www.gutenberg.org/files/6400/6400-h/6400-h.htm.

Tesla, Nikola. 2007a. *My Inventions: The Autobiography of Nikola Tesla*. Radford, VA: Wilder Publications.

———. 2007b. *The Nikola Tesla Treasury*. Radford, VA: Wilder Publications.

Tipuric, Darko. 2014. *Iluzija strategije*. Zagreb: Sinergija.

Tolman, Edward C. 1948. "Cognitive Maps in Rats and Men." *Psychological Review* 55:189–208.

Treisman, Anne, and Daniel Kahneman. 1984. "Changing Views of Attention and Automaticity." In *Varieties of Attention*, edited by R. Parasuraman and R. Davies, 29–61. New York: Academic Press.

Tsoukas, Haridimos, and Robert Chia. 2002. "On Organizational Becoming: Rethinking Organizational Change." *Organization Science* 13 (5):567–582.

Tsoukas, Haridimos, and Mary Jo Hatch. 2001. "Complex Thinking, Complex Practice: The Case for a Narrative Approach to Organizational Complexity." *Human Relations* 54 (8):979–1013.

Van de Ven, Andrew, and Marshall S. Poole. 2005. "Alternative Approaches for Studying Organizational Change." *Organization Studies* 26 (9):1377–1404.

van der Heijden, Kees. 2005. *Scenarios: The Art of Strategic Conversations*. 2nd ed. Hoboken, NJ: John Wiley & Sons.

Walker, Willard, and James Sarbaugh. 1993. "The Early HIstory of the Cherokee Syllabary." *Ethnohistory* 40 (1):70–94.

Weick, Karl E. 1979. *The Social Psychology of Organizing*. Reading MA: Addison-Wesley.

———. 1989. "Theory Construction As Disciplined Imagination." *Academy of Management Review* 14 (4):516–531.

———. 1995. *Sensemaking in Organizations*. Thousand Oaks: Sage Publications.

———. 2001a. "Enactment Processes in Organizations." In *Making Sense of the Organization*, edited by Karl E. Weick. Malden, MA: Blackwell Publishing.

———. 2001b. "Introduction." In *Making Sense of the Organization*, edited by Karl E. Weick. Malden, MA: Blackwell Publishing.

———. 2001c. "Organizational Redesign and Improvisation." In *Making Sense of the Organization*, edited by Karl E. Weick. Malden, MA: Blackwell Publishing.

———. 2001d. "Sensemaking in Organizations: Small Structures with Large Consequences." In *Making Sense of the Organization*, edited by Karl E. Weick. Malden, MA: Blackwell Publishing.

Weick, Karl E., and Michael G Bougon. 1986. "Organizations as Cognitive Maps: Charting Ways to Success and Failure." In *The Thinking Oganization:Dynamics of Organizational Social Cognition*, edited by H. Sims and D. A. Gioia, 102–135. San Francisco: Jossey-Bass.

Weick, Karl E., and Robert E. Quinn. 1999. "Organizational Change and Development." *Annual Review of Psychology* 50:361–386.

Weil, Simon. 2002. *Gravity and Grace*. London: Routledge.

Whitehead, Alfred Norton. 1997. *Science and the Modern World*. New York: The Free Press.

Wilson, Douglas L. 2013. "Lincoln's Rhetoric." *Journal of the Abraham Lincoln Association* 34 (1):1–17.

Wind, Yoram, Colin Crook, and Robert E. Gunther. 2005. *The Power of Impossible Thinking: Transform the Business of Your Life and the Life of Your Business*. New York: Wharton School Pub.

Wood, Julia T. 2007. " Leadership as Persuasion and Adaptation." In *The Pfeiffer Book of Successful Leadership Development Tools*, edited by Jack Gordon. New Jersey: Pfeiffer.

Yantis, Steven. 1993. "Stimulus-Driven Attentional Capture." *Current Directions in Psychological Science* 2:156–161.

Zimbardo, Philip G., and Richard J. Gerrig. 2002. "Perception." In *Foundations of Cognitive Psychology*, edited by Daniel J. Levitin. Cambridge: MIT Press, 133–188.

Index

abstraction, 98
action, 3, 39, 56–60
adaptive decision, 9, 16
adaptive learning, 40, 53
Aesop, 126
Alcoa, 91
Amazon, 17
Apple, 7, 17, 37, 64, 99
Aquinas, St Thomas, 111–13, 130
arguing, 123, 129, 136
argumentation, 119, 123–4, 131–3
Aristotle, 20, 59, 77, 113, 117, 133
attention, 21, 42, 56, 81, 133

behavioral commitment, 10, 39, 116, 125
beliefs, 27, 49, 116, 123, 127
business model, 13, 20, 64–5

Caesar, Julius, 104
categorization, 44, 56
Ching, Tao Te, 70
Christianity, 18
cognition, 30, 42–5, 47–9, 120
cognitive schema, 61–2
collective, 33, 75–6
committing, 124–5, 134
competence, 40, 44, 59–62
competitive enactment, 35
complex organization, 27, 69, 127
complex systems, 25, 38
cooperation, 80, 122
Copernican revolution, 99

courage, 73, 77, 78, 130
creativity, 22, 86, 107

disciplined imagination, 90

emotional disturbance, 63, 72
enactment, 17, 20, 22, 31–3, 67–8, 128
ethos, 20–1
expectation setting, 123, 129, 131
expecting, 123

faith, 78–80
flow of experience, 21, 29, 32, 69–70, 92–7
fortitude, 80, 112
Foucault, Michael, 130
freedom, 75, 111, 130

governing metaphor, 7–9, 17, 18, 20–2, 72, 80–1, 91–5, 98–104, 106–8

hope, 9–10, 20, 21, 78, 103, 110–15
human understanding, 45–6, 49, 93–5
humbleness, 80
Hume, David, 86, 94

IBM, 17
identification, 22, 37, 48–9
identity, 16–7, 20–2, 63, 65–6, 74–81, 112–13
innovation, 38, 86, 97–8

interacion, 18, 26, 28–31, 38–9,
interpretation, 27–33, 37–9, 46–7, 50–2, 89, 120
irrational optimism, 63, 81–3

James, William, 58, 91, 94–5
Jobs, Steve, 52, 57, 64–5, 71, 81, 107, 109, 120
justice, 112

learning process, 54–5
levels of knowledge, 62
Lincoln, Abraham, 72, 117–20
loadstar, 84–7, 89–91, 97–102, 106–8, 128
Locke, John, 59, 86
logical thinking, 34
loyalty, 63, 77, 79, 82–3

managerial and organizational cognition, 36, 42–5
managerial discretion, 34
manipulation, 32, 42, 116, 125–6, 129–31
memory, 46–7, 50, 96
mental map see mental model
mental model, 12, 21, 41, 48–9, 51, 65–73, 93, 107–11
mental shema, 32, 95
metaphor, 20–2, 36–7, 88–104, 113–14
Microsoft, 17, 95
Miller, George, 43

narratives, 85, 89, 122
new, 52–6, 58–60, 63–5, 67–73, 84–90
Nissan Motors, 19
noticing, 100, 102

objectivity, 24–6
observation, 38, 47–9, 55, 57, 59, 108
organization adaptive, 5, 19
organization leaderless, 19
organization navigated, 19
organization radical, 19
organizational adaptation, 34
organizational change, 17–18, 35–6, 74–5, 121–2, 128

organizational mind, 30
organizational research, 25, 27, 29, 92

parrhesia, 22, 129–34
perception, 25, 33, 35, 46–51, 53, 55–8, 73–4
perceptual research, 58
perseverance, 80
personal developement theory, 6, 40
power, 26, 30, 32–3, 68, 81, 121–2, 124–5
pride, 79, 81
problem solving, 15, 18, 47, 49, 52, 59–61, 92–3, 97–8
prudence, 112

radical change in society, 18, 89
radical change individual, 16–18
radical change industrial, 16–18, 34
recognition, 48–9, 56, 87, 96
reflection, 24, 59–60, 94, 107, 125
reflection-in-action, 60
reflection-on-action, 60
resistance to change, 116, 122
rhetoric, 12, 16, 21, 32, 39, 58, 116–34
rhetoric based on action, 10, 125
rhetoric based on beliefs, 10, 123
risk taking, 72–4, 82, 115
roles of the leader, 25–6, 30, 50, 65, 67, 102

scenario, 42, 44, 61, 74, 109
selective attention, 93, 95, 97–101
sensegiving, 37–9, 69–70, 123, 128
sensemaking, 20, 35–9, 66, 68–70, 72–3, 90–3, 101, 104
simplification, 23–4, 39
Simon, Herbert, 16, 28, 43–4
social norms, 14, 122
status quo mental model, 10, 93, 116
strategic management, 33–4, 57

technology, 17, 35, 64, 109
temperance, 112
Tesla, Nikola, 40–2, 61, 66, 68
the French Revolution, 18

transdisciplinary, 52
truth, 41, 46, 58, 88, 112, 121, 129–33

uncertainty, 27, 41, 54, 77, 108

validation of radical mental model, 103, 110

Whitehead, Alfred North, 95

CPSIA information can be obtained at www.ICGtesting.com
Printed in the USA
LVOW10*0006240315

431750LV00006B/30/P

9 781137 492302